Sips & Apps

Sips & Apps

CLASSIC AND CONTEMPORARY RECIPES
FOR COCKTAILS AND APPETIZERS

by Kathy Casey

Photographs by Angie Norwood Browne

CHRONICLE BOOKS

SAN FRANCISCO

Text copyright © 2009 by Kathy Casey.
Photographs copyright © 2009
    by Angie Norwood Browne.
All rights reserved. No part of this book
may be reproduced in any form without
written permission from the publisher.

Library of Congress Cataloging-in-Publication Data:

Casey, Kathy.
    Sips and apps : classic and contemporary recipes for
cocktails and appetizers / by Kathy Casey ; photographs
by Angie Norwood Browne.
        p. cm.
    Includes index.
    ISBN 978-0-8118-6406-0 (hardcover)
    1. Cocktails. 2. Appetizers. I. Title.
TX951.C345 2009
641.8'74—dc22

                        20083344

Manufactured in China.

Designed and typeset by Gretchen Scoble
Edited by Ann E. Manly
Food styling by Charlotte Omnès and Patty Wittmann

10 9 8 7 6 5 4 3 2 1

Chronicle Books LLC
680 Second Street
San Francisco, California 94107
www.chroniclebooks.com

Front cover:
Pear Thyme Fizz (page 48), Piccolo Caprese Picks
with Quick Basil Aioli (page 154), and Cha Cha
Cashews (page 142)

Raw eggs and raw or undercooked fish, shellfish, and other animal products are not recommended for pregnant women, children, the elderly, or anyone with immune deficiencies.

I would like to dedicate this book
to John Casey, my love, my husband,
my personal supporter, and my chief taste-tester.
Thank you for our delicious life together.

Contents

Acknowledgments

In creating a new dish or drink, it's not just one "thing" that makes it great but a culmination of ideas and flavors. Likewise, it takes the tribulations, trials, and lots of tastings by many talented people to produce a book. To begin, I would like to thank my longtime associate and dear friend, Ann Manly, for her patient and spot-on editing expertise and for always keeping my voice so clear, and executive sous-chef Matthew Noesen and associate Mary-Elizabeth Crowe for their testing assistance and tasting talents. Thanks, also, to John, Trixie, Alex, and Dave for being willing tasters. Also much thanks goes to Chronicle Books: to my editor, Bill LeBlond, for believing in this book and for his creative insights; to editor Amy Treadwell for her guidance and support; and to the rest of the Chronicle folks for their enthusiasm and commitment.

I am deeply grateful as well to the dedicated team that brought the pages of this book to life: to photographer Angie Norwood Browne for her beautiful and stunning photography; to Charlotte Omnès and Patty Wittmann for their creative and skillful food styling; and to designer Gretchen Scoble for her artful eye and gift for bringing together the work and talents of everyone so beautifully and stylishly.

Great thanks also goes to the many spirit companies that I work with every day and particularly to Absolut and Beam Global, Bacardi, Brown-Forman, and Crown Imports for supporting my work on this book.

I also want to thank the bartenders and mixologists who are making it happen every day as well as the many dedicated cocktail enthusiasts. They have all helped to bring the craft of the cocktail back to the prominence it so deserves.

Introduction

As a chef, I am always trying new things—and not only in the kitchen. My mantra has long been, "A great drink is just as important as a great dish." Bringing culinary ingredients and a fresh-and-seasonal philosophy into the bar has helped to make that a reality. I may very well be the first Bar Chef!

Inventing signature cocktails—whether for a cruise line, luxury hotel, chef's bistro, or spirit brand—is a big part of my business. It's what I have been doing for many years now, so it's exciting to see how the creative cocktails trend has taken off. Making drinks is really liquid cooking, where the bar is a Liquid Kitchen. A well-crafted cocktail has as much thought put into it and requires the same balancing of flavors—in this case liquor and modifiers—as a dish from the kitchen. And not only are innovative cocktails being shaken up, but the old and overlooked classics have made a grand comeback as well.

Of course people want to re-create the beverages they've enjoyed in bars and restaurants and share them with friends at home. And what's an extraordinary drink without a fantastic nibble to go with it? How often do you go out to eat or to a party and the entire "meal" is appetizers and cocktails? It's often the way we eat, sip, and entertain today. Every sip needs a d'lish app!

My philosophy in entertaining is simple: don't overdo it. Pick one or two signature cocktails for your get-together, select a few appetizers—being sure to have a good variety of hot and cold—and make as much in advance as you can.

So, whether you're throwing a big cocktail party or inviting a few neighbors over, I hope that these recipes will bring you years of enjoyment and become your new favorite sips and apps.

P.S. Enjoy yourself but always remember to drink responsibly.

GENERAL RECIPE NOTES FOR SIPS & APPS

When trying a recipe for the first time, be sure to read it all the way through before starting. When making drinks, set your bar area with ice, tools, and glasses. Next, get all your ingredients out and be ready to mix. When cooking, I like to cut, prepare, and measure ingredients ahead of time, basically making a "kit," then double-check my work one last time and proceed from there.

Cooking and mixing drinks are arts, not sciences. Many variables contribute to the results: ingredients from different producers and parts of the country vary, ovens and burner strengths differ, etc. Use your best judgment and rely on your own sensibilities when making the recipes in this book.

REPERTOIRE FOR TODAY'S BAR

Spirits

High-quality spirits are imperative for a well-stocked bar. But with all the choices today, making your selection can be a daunting task. I recommend getting the basics and then acquiring more out-of-the-ordinary bottles a few at a time or when the "spirit moves you"! Unusual liquors can be a welcome hostess gift to take to a party or even to request that guests bring to yours.

Here is my list of spirit basics, but you may want to tailor it to what your friends and guests drink:

bourbon
brandy
gin
rum (white)
Scotch
tequila
triple sec or other orange-flavored liqueur
vermouth (both dry white and sweet red)
vodka

The next tier:

rum (dark or spiced)
rye whiskey
vodka (premium and flavored)
whiskey (premium)

And a variety of liqueurs, such as some of my favorites:

Chambord—a French berry liqueur
Amarula Cream—a cream liqueur made from the South African marula fruit
Tuaca—an Italian liqueur with hints of orange, vanilla, and butterscotch
Frangelico—an Italian hazelnut liqueur
Campari—a pleasantly bitter Italian aperitif infused with more than sixty ingredients
Pernod—a French, anise-flavored liqueur

Fruits & Vegetables

Fruits and vegetables have been incorporated into spirits for centuries. Fruit in sangria dates back to Roman times, and vegetables have been brewed up in digestifs by Italian monks since the Middle Ages. Today, fresh fruits and vegetables can inspire fantastic seasonal cocktails.

Always rinse fresh fruits or vegetables before using in drinks, and purchase organic whenever possible.

Celery and cucumber have long contributed their fresh crunch to classics such as the Bloody Mary and Pimm's Cup. Celery certainly adds a unique crisp dry quality to my Celery 'N' Tonic (page 76), and cucumbers bring a fresh accent, especially to cocktails based on Asian liquors, such as my So' Fresh (page 39) made with Korean soju. In cocktails, I like to use regular cucumbers, rather than the English hothouse variety, for their more pronounced flavor; and I also keep the skin on for its extra flavor and color.

Bell peppers can get into the action with their distinctive savor when muddled into citrus-based cocktails, and hot peppers deliver that little bit of "zip," as in the Hot Mango Love (page 40). The heat of hot peppers varies significantly, so use care when incorporating them.

Fresh ginger, beets, and horseradish are always peeled.

Tree fruits, such as apples and pears, are not peeled. Fruits with fuzzy skin, such as peach or kiwifruit, or with thick rind, such as pineapple, watermelon, or cantaloupe, are peeled unless otherwise specified. Frozen fruits can be substituted if stated in the recipe.

Homemade fruit purees can be stored, refrigerated, for up to 5 days or, frozen, for up to 6 months. I like to make purees when fruits are at their seasonal peaks and freeze them in small amounts for off-season mixing.

Citrus

Citrus fruits are the most extensively used in the bar, so I am treating them separately. Citrus is not peeled for use in cocktails; in fact, the oil from the peel can be
as important as the juice. Always be sure to wash your citrus.

FRESH CITRUS JUICES These are imperative and provide a vibrant flavor "pop"
to drinks. When juicing fresh citrus, bring the fruit to room temperature and roll
it on a counter before juicing to extract the maximum amount of juice. Fresh citrus
juices are often available in the produce department of well-stocked grocers. If
you are going to be using a lot of citrus juice, I recommend getting a hand-cranked
citrus juicer to make the task easy. Otherwise, a reamer makes a small juicing job
easier. Be sure to measure citrus juices with a jigger because even a little too much
or too little can seriously alter your drink.

I like to put juices in pretty glass bottles. Citrus juice is best used the day it is
squeezed, but it can be stored, refrigerated, for up to 3 days.

CUTTING CITRUS Cut citrus the day you intend to use it, not too far in advance.
Always use a sharp or serrated knife.

To make wedges, cut a lemon, lime,
orange, or grapefruit in half lengthwise, and then cut each half lengthwise into 4 wedges. Each whole fruit
yields 8 wedges.

To cut lemon, lime, or orange
wheels, cut the ends off the fruit and
discard. Then cut the fruit crosswise
into 1/4-inch-thick slices. A medium
lemon or lime yields 6 wheels; a
medium orange yields 8 wheels.

Herbs

I have been incorporating fresh herbs into my cocktails for years, so I'm pleased to see the aromatic sprigs (beyond mint) mentioned now on so many drink lists. It's about time herbs made their way to the bar!

Fresh herbs can totally modify a cocktail's profile, adding that subtle difference that makes it a "Wow!" Take, for instance, fresh sage: its dusky character marries well with tequila when shaken into a margarita.

When using fresh herbs, be sure to give them a light rinse. And, unless the stems are very large, keep them on! Herb stems contain a ton of flavor, and you want it all to come alive in your cocktail. Always bend or tear herbs before dropping them into your cocktail shaker so that the aromatic oils are more easily released. If shaking herbs in, be sure to shake your cocktail extra hard. If muddling, press gently with a muddler, then build the drink.

When setting up your bar, keep fresh herbs like you would a small flower arrangement. They look stylish in tiny vases or glasses one-third filled with water.

Some of my favorite herbs for cocktails:

Sage—Splendid mixed with tangerine, other citrus, or tequila or in a
   brandy sidecar.

Thyme—Delicious with pear, apple, or gin-based drinks.

Basil—A natural shaken with Bloody Marys or strawberry-based drinks.
   Lovely with lemonade or with mint, in a fresh cherry mojito.

Rosemary—Complements lemon, apple, pear, or grapefruit.

Tarragon—Its slightly anise flavor is perfect with peach. I especially love
   tarragon mixed with gin.

Lemon Verbena—This fragrant herb is grown mostly in home gardens. It is
   splendid with berry-based drinks and pairs naturally with lemon or
   other citrus. Best mixed with clear spirits, such as vodka, gin, or
   white rum.

Mint—This herbal workhorse is traditional with bourbon or chocolate
   drinks as well as with rum, gin, and vodka.

Cilantro—Excellent muddled with melon or cucumber and mixes well with
   tequila, white rum, or vodka.

Bitters

Why use bitters? What will they do for a cocktail? I like to say that bitters are the salt and pepper of the bar. These age-old extractions are typically made from herbs, spices, and citrus dissolved in alcohol or glycerin and taste bitter or bittersweet. Bitters provide roundness and a "seasoning-like" enhancement to a drink. When you make a cocktail and you think, "It's just missing something," next time add just a dash of bitters . . . a little goes a long way.

There are many types of bitters, from the familiar Angostura and Peychaud's to Regans' Orange Bitters No. 6 and Fee Brothers' multiple varieties. If you'd like to experiment, then gather a few and add a dash to your favorite cocktail to see how they differ.

Sweeteners & Sours

SIMPLE SYRUP This is a bar staple and the most commonly used sweetener. Though you can purchase simple syrup, it is ordinarily sweeter than I prefer, so I highly recommend making your own. Proportions vary but it is easy. The cocktails in this book are made with the following recipe.

Simple Syrup

MAKES 3 CUPS

> 2 cups water
>
> 2 cups sugar

Mix the water and sugar together in a small saucepan and bring to a boil over medium-high heat. Let boil 1 minute, then immediately remove from the heat. Let cool to room temperature before using. Store in a clean glass bottle or container, at room temperature, for up to 2 weeks or, refrigerated, for up to 3 months.

OTHER SWEETENERS These include Clover Honey Syrup (page 93) and agave nectar (see page 199), also known as agave syrup, which is made from the juice of the Mexican agave plant and is popular as a sweetener in margaritas or as an alternative to simple syrup.

SOURS Today's bar demands fresh, high-quality sweet-and-sour. Typically, a sour is one part lemon or lime (or half lemon and half lime) juice to one part simple syrup.

Most of the recipes in this book break out the components of lemon or lime juice and simple syrup for the ease of making a few drinks at a moment's notice. For a drink that you may be doing for a crowd, such as the Douglas Fir Sparkletini (page 50) or Poppy's Margarita (page 79), I have included a large-batch recipe so that the sour can be prepared in advance. This makes for easy measurement when mixing multiple drinks.

Some of the drinks in this book use the following sour recipe; I'm sure you'll find many additional uses for it as well.

Fresh Lemon-Lime Sour

MAKES 2 CUPS

½ cup fresh lemon juice

½ cup fresh lime juice

1 cup Simple Syrup (page 19)

In a medium container or pitcher with a lid, combine the ingredients. Cover and keep refrigerated for up to 2 weeks.

To make a Fresh Lemon Sour or a Fresh Lime Sour variation: use all fresh lemon juice or all fresh lime juice.

Sugars & Salts

SUGAR RIMS Sugar rims are a must-do for drinks such as lemon drops or sidecars. Sugar rims can also incorporate other flavors, such as rosemary in the Tuscan Rosemary Lemon Drop (page 47). It is essential to use superfine or baker's sugar for rimming glasses as regular granulated sugar is too coarse and not as meltingly sexy on the lips.

I like to make a very deep sugar rim, which is a bit different from the standard. A standard sugar rim is made by dipping the edge of the glass rim into simple syrup and then into sugar. My deeper rim looks beautiful and makes a dramatic statement when you rim a large quantity of glasses in advance and stack them up on your bar—ready to be filled!

To make a deep sugar rim: Set out a wide bowl filled with superfine sugar. Holding a martini glass by the stem, press a lemon or orange wedge against the top 1 to 1½ inches of the outside rim of the glass and rotate the glass to coat the rim lightly with juice. Then push the rim into the bowl of sugar at a 45-degree angle. Spin the glass until the outside moistened area is completely and evenly coated with sugar. Holding the glass upside down, tap lightly to remove excess sugar. Do not get sugar inside the glass. Glasses can be pre-sugared up to one day in advance.

SALT RIMS Kosher salt is the salt most frequently used for rimming glasses. Although you can purchase "margarita salts," I prefer the clean taste of kosher salt. Salt rims are most common for margaritas, Bloody Marys, and cheladas. Salts can also be seasoned with such ingredients as celery seed, black pepper, or chipotle chile powder.

To make a salt rim: Set out a wide bowl filled with kosher salt. Holding your glass at the bottom, wipe a lemon or orange wedge against the top outer rim. Then dip it into the salt and rotate the glass to completely coat the outside rim with a small amount of salt. Keeping the glass upside down, tap lightly to remove excess salt. Do not get salt inside the glass. I also like to offer guests drinks with a "half rim" of salt.

Ice

Ice is a very important element in cocktail making. First, you want to have plenty as you never want to run out! And be sure your ice tastes "fresh" since this can really affect your finished drink. Ice from grocery or convenience stores and from home-refrigerator automatic ice machines is usually larger than ideal for shaking cocktails. These big cubes do not break up as much as smaller ones. There is not much you can do about this unless you have a friendly restaurant that will give you ice for your next party. Other alternatives are to break up bigger cubes with an ice mallet or get trays that make small-sized cubes. Last, but probably most important of all, is keeping your ice drained. I like to keep my ice in a big colander in the sink and refresh my ice bucket often.

Garnishes

Garnishes are that extra something that can make a cocktail more dashing or beautiful. I liken a garnish to a pretty piece of jewelry on a little black dress. Garnishes need not be extravagant: a single cranberry floating in a cosmo gives it an elegant edge, and a lime wheel poked through the center with a straw is whimsical in a margarita. The embellishment should always echo the ingredients in the cocktail—however, paper parasols are sometimes approved. . . .

LONG CITRUS-ZEST TWISTS Twists can be made with any kind of citrus fruit and are best "zested" directly over the drink so that all the tasty oils spritz into the cocktail.

To make a citrus-zest twist: Using a channel knife (see page 199), cut into the citrus peel, removing a strip around the fruit at least 3 to 4 inches long, then twist the strip and artfully hang it into or across the drink.

CITRUS WEDGES & WHEELS These are always best when freshly cut (see page 15).

FRUITS Whether it be a fresh raspberry to float in your drink or a strawberry to adorn the rim, choose the best fruit available. Pears, apples, peaches, apricots, and nectarines tend to brown when cut, so, for garnish, cut these per drink as needed. Shave fresh coconut with a potato peeler. Fresh pineapple, mango, watermelon, and other melons can be cut into long spears.

CHERRIES Old-school maraschino cherries are a must-have-on-hand item as some people still prefer them in timeless drinks, such as manhattans. But these days, I like to make spirited cherries by plumping big dried sweet cherries in liquor (see page 75). It's easy to do and they keep well.

OLIVES I've been known to serve up an occasional kalamata or cerignola olive in a martini though many die-hard classic-martini drinkers expect a traditional pimiento-stuffed green olive. But with so many tasty variations available, it's nice to stock an assortment. My favorites are stuffed with garlic or blue cheese.

PICKLEY THINGS & VEGGIES Pickled vegetables make tasty cocktail garnishes. Grace a martini or Bloody Mary with pickled asparagus, green beans, tiny green tomatoes, or large caperberries with stems. When garnishing with fresh celery, choose the small crisp inside stalks with a little leaf. Baby carrots and cucumbers—from thin wheels to spears—also make delicious garnishes.

FRESH HERBS When garnishing with fresh herbs, use small, very perky leaves or sprigs. I like to float the herb or lay it across the top of the drink so that you get that nose hit before your first sip.

UNIQUE GARNISHES When a drink is for a special occasion, go all out. For example, you could float a single, large, non-sprayed white rose petal on a wedding cocktail or sprinkle edible glitter over whipped cream on a hot-coffee drink. I've even used a glow-stick-bracelet garnish at a women's party where the theme was illumination!

BAR EQUIPMENT & GLASSWARE

Equipment

Having good, basic equipment is a must for those who love to shake, swizzle, and stir. But this does not mean that you have to spend loads of money. My favorite tools are those purchased from restaurant-supply stores (see page 199). Good equipment is worth the investment and will last through years of use.

SHAKERS There are basically two types, the standard three-piece shaker that has a canister, a lid with a built-in strainer, and a cap; and the Boston-style shaker, which is my favorite. It consists of a mixing glass and a stainless-steel canister. This style does not come with a strainer, so you need to purchase one separately. I prefer this setup because I like to build the drink in the clear mixing glass so all the beautiful ingredients show through.

STRAINERS Most widely used is a Hawthorne strainer, which is circular and has a spring coil. Usually it is fitted into the metal half of a Boston shaker for straining, but I prefer to strain from the clear mixing glass in order to show off the contents, especially when the drink contains fruit or herb pieces.

JIGGERS Typical metal two-sided jiggers have one side measuring 1, 1½, or 2 ounces and the other side measuring ½, ¾, or 1 ounce. I recommend getting at least two sizes to cover a range. Fancy jiggers without clear markings are not recommended. See page 28 for measuring tips.

MUDDLERS These bat-like tools, about 10 inches long and customarily made of wood or plastic, are used for crushing or muddling fruits and herbs. (If you do not have a muddler, you can use a wooden spoon or other blunt-end kitchen utensil.) My favorite muddlers come from Mr. Mojito (see page 199).

OTHER ESSENTIALS

Pour spouts

Channel knife for zesting

Long-handled bar spoon

Assorted picks, swizzle sticks, and straws

Ice bucket and small scoop or tongs

Pitchers in various sizes for holding fresh juices

Pretty, clear bottles for bottling premixes, simple syrup, or infusions

Glassware

There are hundreds of choices when it comes to glasses. Over the years, I have found myself collecting way too many glasses and then using only a favorite few. So now I say, keep it simple. If you entertain often at home, you might want to purchase restaurant-grade glasses by the case as they are very durable and inexpensive. Inquire at a restaurant-supply store in your area; most will sell to you.

My favorite basic glasses follow:

MARTINI GLASS, ALSO KNOWN AS A COCKTAIL GLASS Martini glasses can range from 4 to 8 ounces in capacity. I like to use the smaller glasses for vodka or gin martinis and larger ones for "up" cocktails that contain more ingredients. Collecting martini glasses—mixing and matching them—is also a fun way to acquire enough to serve a large group.

TALL GLASS, ALSO KNOWN AS A COLLINS GLASS OR HIGHBALL GLASS Tall and thin, this type of glass ranges from 8 to 14 ounces in volume. You may want to have two sizes, and gauge the glass to the drink accordingly.

OLD-FASHIONED GLASS, ALSO KNOWN AS A BUCKET GLASS OR ROCKS GLASS A short squat glass, generally with a thick base. The volume ranges from 6 to 8 ounces, or larger for double old-fashioned glasses.

LARGE GLASS, ALSO KNOWN AS A PINT GLASS This type of glass holds between 14 and 16 ounces and is for large-volume drinks.

CHAMPAGNE FLUTE A stemmed tall slender glass ranging from 6 to 8 ounces in volume. The shape is good for keeping the bubbles in.

WINE GLASS Stemmed wine glasses are not only for wine. Oversized wine glasses make an interesting choice for serving sangrias or juice-based drinks on the rocks.

SHOT GLASS Shot glasses, especially oversized, tall, or uniquely shaped ones, make a cool vehicle to serve "tastes" of drinks or mini dessert drinks.

CORDIAL OR LIQUEUR GLASS These small glasses hold from 1 to 3 ounces. I like to put out my collection of one-of-a-kind tiny glasses with a selection of liqueurs and cordials for after-dinner sips.

Getting creative

Sometimes it's fun to get out an assortment of liquors, mixers, and other ingredients and let your creative juices flow. Get a flavor concept going; perhaps use a classic or favorite as your model to work from. Maybe a visit to the farmers' market is your inspiration, or an interesting drink you had last night at a restaurant. Unleash your imagination and start mixing.

Be sure to write down what you do so that, if you love it, you can re-create it. Or, if not, change it up and try again. That is how great cocktails are invented.

When taste-testing your drink, be sure, most of all, that the flavors are balanced. When they are, you will know it: as you take that first sip, a smile will slowly spread across your lips. And that's cocktail magic!

Measuring

Measuring is as important in the bar as it is in the kitchen. When making cocktails with strong liquors, sweetening agents, or citrus juices, being a little off can make a huge difference, so I highly recommend using a jigger.

Bar Measurements, Equivalents & Handy Yield Information

When reading bar recipes and measuring liquids in the bar, an ounce means a fluid ounce.

$\frac{1}{8}$ ounce = $\frac{3}{4}$ teaspoon

$\frac{1}{4}$ ounce = 1$\frac{1}{2}$ teaspoons

$\frac{1}{2}$ ounce = 1 tablespoon

1 ounce = 2 tablespoons

1$\frac{1}{2}$ ounces = 3 tablespoons

2 ounces = 4 tablespoons ($\frac{1}{4}$ cup)

3 ounces = 6 tablespoons

4 ounces = 8 tablespoons ($\frac{1}{2}$ cup)

6 ounces = 12 tablespoons ($\frac{3}{4}$ cup)

8 ounces = 16 tablespoons (1 cup)

750 ml bottle = 25.4 ounces (generous 3 cups)

1-liter bottle = 33.8 ounces (about 4$\frac{1}{4}$ cups)

1 medium lime = 1 ounce (2 tablespoons) juice

1 medium lemon = 1$\frac{1}{2}$ ounces (3 tablespoons) juice

1 medium orange = 2$\frac{1}{2}$ to 3 ounces juice

1 medium grapefruit = 6 ounces juice

Muddling

Place the ingredients to be muddled, such as fruits or herbs, directly into a cocktail shaker. Do not add ice yet. Using a muddler, press down on the ingredients a few times, giving it some force but not too much muscle. You want to extract the essences not pulverize the items.

Building a Cocktail

For cocktails that will be shaken, start with a cocktail shaker. First, put in any solid components, such as citrus wedges (their juice may be squeezed in before dropping in the rind), fresh herbs, or items to be muddled. If muddling, do so before adding ice. Next, fill the shaker at least three quarters full with ice. Measure in the liquors, juices, sweeteners, and accents, such as bitters.

If building a cocktail in the glass it is to be served in, fill it with ice to the rim (unless otherwise specified). Measure in the ingredients and stir with a bar spoon.

SHAKING Once the cocktail is built, place the shaker tin over the mixing glass or the cap on the cocktail shaker, secure, and shake vigorously for about 6 seconds.

Proper shaking both chills the cocktail and also dilutes it slightly to soften and balance its flavors.

STIRRING After building the cocktail in the mixing glass or shaker, insert a long bar spoon and twist it back and forth while moving it up and down. Always stir for at least 20 seconds for optimum chill. Stirring preserves the sparkling transparency of a clear cocktail.

STRAINING Strain the cocktail directly into a serving glass. If the cocktail is served "up," no ice is added to the serving glass. If "on the rocks," fill the serving glass with fresh ice before straining in the drink. Strain quickly, without hesitation, to prevent dribbles.

GARNISHING Garnish the cocktail right before serving. Garnishes can be floated, picked, or laid across or secured on the rim of the glass.

COCKTAIL NO-NO'S Never build more than two cocktails in a shaker at the same time and never reuse ice for shaking.

Premixing

When throwing a big party, who wants to be chained to the bar the whole time? Now premixing is not for a martini or manhattan; it's for cocktails with multiple ingredients. So pick one or two cocktails, then do the math. Multiply the main elements by the number of drinks you want to make. Measure everything out. Mix in a large container, and then put the mixture in attractive bottles or a pretty pitcher. Premix can be held, refrigerated, for up to 5 days. Be sure to shake up or remix well before using. Then all you have to do is shake or stir over ice, ensuring that every one of your cocktails will be precision-perfect.

Fortunella

Lychees have a light floral and white grape–like flavor. This drink is really easy to make and a good choice for a tropical-theme party or to serve with Pacific Rim–influenced dishes such as Asian Shrimp Cakes with Sweet Chili Sauce (page 176).

3 ounces Lychee-Infused Vodka (recipe follows)

FOR GARNISHING
Lychee from the infused vodka

Fill a cocktail shaker with ice. Measure in the infused vodka. Cap and shake vigorously. Strain into a martini glass. Garnish with a lychee.

Lychee-Infused Vodka
MAKES ABOUT 2 ¾ CUPS

1 (20-ounce) can whole seedless lychees in syrup
1½ cups vodka

In a clean glass jar with a tight-fitting lid, mix the lychees and their syrup and vodka. Let infuse, refrigerated, for at least 2 days, or up to 4 weeks, before using.

☛ TIP   This infusion is also delicious with a tiny splash of blue Curaçao added, or made with gin instead of vodka.

Amante Picante

This savory sipper was created by renowned mixologist Francesco Lafranconi, known for his endless innovation. In the bar his motto is "We're not drinking ... we're learning!"

two ¼-inch-thick slices cucumber

5 fresh cilantro leaves

2 ounces Cazadores blanco tequila

1 ounce fresh lime juice

¾ ounce raw organic agave nectar, or substitute Simple Syrup (page 19)

7 drops Tabasco green pepper sauce

FOR GARNISHING

Slice of cucumber

In a cocktail shaker, press the cucumber slices and cilantro with a muddler to release the flavors. Fill the shaker with ice. Measure in the tequila, lime juice, and agave nectar. Add the Tabasco. Cap and shake vigorously. Strain into a martini glass. Garnish with a cucumber slice on the rim.

Red Square Martini

Shaking in a thin slice of fresh beet adds such a beautiful color and the merest sugges-
tion of earthiness. With simply the lemon-twist garnish, this drink is lovely with the
Mini Scallion Biscuits with Smoked Salmon Spread & Pickled Onions (page 156).

Dash of dry white vermouth

2 ounces vodka, preferably Russian

1 tiny slice peeled raw beet (about the size of a quarter)

FOR GARNISHING

Long lemon-zest twist

Tiny slice of cold-smoked salmon

Tiny sprig of fresh dill

Roll the vermouth around in a cocktail shaker, then shake out any excess.
Fill the shaker with ice. Measure in the vodka. Drop in the beet. Cap and shake
vigorously. Strain into a martini glass.

Zest the lemon over the cocktail and drop the lemon twist in the drink. Thread
the salmon onto a skewer or pick, lay it across the drink, then place the dill
sprig on the salmon.

So' Fresh

Soju is a Korean spirit distilled from sweet potatoes, and it packs a powerful punch. Refreshing cucumber makes this the ultimate drink with Asian foods, especially sushi. Accompany with California Crab "Truffles" (page 184) or Soy-Glazed Seared Tuna on Green Onion Pancakes (page 168).

3 slices cucumber

2 ounces soju or vodka

¾ ounce fresh lime juice

½ ounce Simple Syrup (page 19)

Small splash of chilled soda water

FOR GARNISHING

Thin slice of cucumber

In a cocktail shaker, press the 3 cucumber slices with a muddler to release their flavor. Fill the shaker with ice. Measure in the soju, lime juice, and simple syrup. Cap and shake vigorously. Strain into a martini glass. Add a splash of soda water. Garnish with a cucumber slice.

Hot Mango Love

Good friend and ingenious mixologist Ryan Magarian created this cocktail while working with me on a bar project. He has a true gift for melding unique flavor combinations as well as for giving his drinks playful names.

1 to 2 thin slices fresh jalapeño pepper

1½ ounces Finlandia mango vodka

¾ ounce fresh lemon juice

½ ounce fresh orange juice

½ ounce Simple Syrup (page 19)

2 dashes Fee Brothers peach bitters

FOR GARNISHING

Thin slice of fresh jalapeño pepper

Drop the jalapeño slices into a cocktail shaker. Fill the shaker with ice. Measure in the vodka, lemon and orange juices, and simple syrup. Add the bitters. Cap and shake vigorously. Strain into a martini glass. Float a jalapeño slice in the drink for garnish.

Rouge Pulp

I created this cocktail on the fly when I was on a total bourbon kick and just happened to have a bunch of blood oranges. My imbibing partners pronounced it spectacular. While brainstorming what to call it, one of my girlfriends whipped out her new lipstick and cried out, "Rouge Pulp!" Thus the drink was officially christened.

⅛ Ruby Red or pink grapefruit

¼ blood orange, or, if not in season, substitute another orange

2 ounces bourbon

¾ ounce sweet red vermouth

1 teaspoon juice from jarred maraschino cherries

FOR GARNISHING
Maraschino cherry with stem

Squeeze the grapefruit and orange into a cocktail shaker and drop in. Fill the shaker with ice. Measure in the bourbon, vermouth, and cherry juice. Cap and shake vigorously. Strain into a martini glass or serve on the rocks in an old-fashioned glass. Garnish with a maraschino cherry.

Blue Thai Mojito

MAKES 1 DRINK

The infused syrup adds an exotic kick to this tall rum drink. Pair this intriguing cocktail with Seared Thai Beef Lettuce Cups with Lemongrass & Lime (page 158).

¼ ounce blue Curaçao

1½ ounces Bacardi Limon rum or Bacardi white rum

1½ ounces Coco-Mint Syrup (recipe follows)

1 ounce fresh lime juice

2 ounces chilled soda water

FOR GARNISHING

Fresh mint and/or cilantro sprigs

Shaved coconut (optional)

Fill a tall glass with ice. Measure in the Curaçao, rum, syrup, lime juice, and soda water. Stir with a bar spoon. Garnish with fresh mint and/or cilantro and a sprinkling of shaved coconut, if using.

Coco-Mint Syrup

MAKES 3 CUPS, ENOUGH FOR ABOUT 16 DRINKS

1 cup shredded sweetened coconut

¼ teaspoon red pepper flakes

1 bunch fresh mint, torn

12 large sprigs fresh cilantro

2 cups sugar

2 cups water

Combine the ingredients in a medium saucepan and bring to a boil. Boil for 2 to 3 minutes. Remove from the heat and let steep for 1 hour. Strain, pressing out as much liquid as possible, then discard the solids. Let cool to room temperature. If not using immediately, cover and refrigerate, for up to 1 month, until needed. Remix before using.

Grapefruit Cosmo

It's the pink drink even men will drink. The cosmo is a new classic; its flavor profile opens it to many variations, as in this version where grapefruit vodka goes splendidly with the cranberry juice. For a clear cosmo, make this drink with white cranberry juice. Warm Brie & Almond Crostini with Harvest Apple Chutney (page 191) is a natural pairing as the tanginess of the drink counterbalances the creamy brie. Orange Pistachio Cocktail Cookies (page 172) also complement this cosmo.

1½ ounces Absolut Ruby Red grapefruit vodka

½ ounce triple sec

¾ ounce fresh lime juice

1 ounce cranberry juice

FOR GARNISHING

Fresh or frozen cranberry

Fill a cocktail shaker with ice. Measure in the vodka, triple sec, and lime and cranberry juices. Cap and shake vigorously. Strain into a martini glass. Float a cranberry in the drink for garnish.

Tuscan Rosemary Lemon Drop

I created this cocktail for the wedding reception of my dear friends Michelle and Don, in Tuscany. I can still picture everyone on the villa lawn enjoying their drinks—heels kicked off, ties loosened, and laughter fading into the sunset.

Rosemary Sugar (recipe follows)

1 sprig fresh rosemary

1½ ounces vodka

½ ounce limoncello

½ ounce fresh lemon juice

½ ounce Simple Syrup (page 19)

FOR GARNISHING
Fresh rosemary sprig

Rim a large martini glass (see page 21) with rosemary sugar, and set aside.

Bend 1 rosemary sprig and drop into a cocktail shaker. Fill the shaker with ice. Measure in the vodka, limoncello, lemon juice, and simple syrup. Cap and shake vigorously. Strain into the sugar-rimmed glass. Float a rosemary sprig in the drink for garnish.

Rosemary Sugar

MAKES 1 CUP

2 tablespoons fresh rosemary leaves, coarsely chopped

1 cup superfine or baker's sugar

Mix the rosemary and sugar together in a small bowl, and spread the mixture on a rimmed baking sheet. Set in a warm dry place for about 4 days, until the rosemary is completely dried. Process in a food processor or spice grinder until finely ground. Store in a tightly sealed container for up to 1 month at room temperature.

☛ TIP   If you don't have limoncello, increase the lemon juice and simple syrup to ¾ ounce each.

Pear Thyme Fizz

Fresh thyme's savoriness is wonderful against the crisp dryness of pear. Accompanied by Roasted Pear Crostini with Gorgonzola (page 197), this sparkling cocktail is pure pear'fection.

1 large sprig fresh thyme

¾ ounce vodka

¾ ounce pear vodka

½ ounce fresh lemon juice

¾ ounce Simple Syrup (page 19)

Splash of chilled brut Champagne, dry sparkling wine, or soda water

FOR GARNISHING

Thin slice of fresh pear

Small sprig of fresh thyme

Bend the large thyme sprig and drop into a cocktail shaker. Fill the shaker with ice. Measure in the vodkas, lemon juice, and simple syrup. Cap and shake vigorously. Strain into a martini glass. Top with a splash of Champagne. Float a pear slice and thyme sprig in the drink for garnish.

Kiwi Caipirinha

Cachaça is a Brazilian liquor distilled from sugarcane juice. If you can't get cachaça, substitute white rum or vodka.

½ large lime, cut into 4 pieces

2 teaspoons sugar

½ large kiwifruit, peeled and cut into 6 chunks

3 ounces cachaça

FOR GARNISHING

Slice of kiwifruit

49

In a cocktail shaker, combine the lime pieces and sugar and press with a muddler to release the juice. Add the kiwifruit and press with muddler to crush. Fill the shaker with ice. Measure in the cachaça. Cap and shake vigorously. Pour into an old-fashioned glass. Garnish with a slice of kiwifruit.

Summer Bourbon Sparkling Cider

Effervescent cider lightens up bourbon for a smooth-sipping summer cocktail. A smidgen of apricot brandy makes it go down easy.

1 lemon wedge

1 ounce bourbon

½ ounce apricot brandy

2 to 3 ounces chilled sparkling apple cider

FOR GARNISHING

Lemon wedge

Squeeze 1 lemon wedge into a tall glass and drop in. Fill the glass with ice. Measure in the bourbon and apricot brandy. Top with sparkling cider and stir gently. Garnish with a lemon wedge.

Douglas Fir Sparkletini

This is absolutely my favorite holiday cocktail. The light essence of Douglas fir infusing the gin evokes a sleigh ride in the woods, and the pouf of Champagne adds a festive effervescence. Serve alongside cheery goat cheese–stuffed D'Lish Peppadew Peppers (page 177).

1½ ounces Douglas Fir–Infused Gin (recipe follows)
¾ ounce white cranberry juice
1½ ounces Fresh Lemon Sour (page 20)
Splash of brut Champagne or dry sparkling wine

FOR GARNISHING
Tiny sprig of Douglas fir
Fresh or frozen cranberry

Fill a cocktail shaker with ice. Measure in the infused gin, cranberry juice, and lemon sour. Cap and shake vigorously. Strain into a martini glass and top with a splash of Champagne. Garnish with a fir sprig and float a cranberry in the drink.

Douglas Fir–Infused Gin

MAKES ENOUGH FOR ABOUT 16 DRINKS

1 (5- to 6-inch) sprig fresh-picked Douglas fir branch, rinsed
1 (750 ml) bottle gin

Put the fir branch into the gin bottle, cap, and let sit 24 hours. (Do not let it infuse for more than 24 hours.) Remove the branch and discard. The infused gin can be stored at room temperature for up to 1 year.

☛ TIP   If fresh Douglas fir is not available in your area, then you can substitute a Douglas fir tea bag (see page 199). If using the tea, add the contents of the tea bag to the gin, let infuse, and then strain the gin through a very fine strainer. The infused gin also makes a good martini.

Strawberry Shag

Fresh basil lends a fun flavor note to the classic combination of strawberries and lemonade. Soda water introduces a lively sparkle.

1 to 2 large sprigs fresh basil
¼ cup Sugared Strawberries, with juice (recipe follows)
1½ ounces vodka
1 ounce fresh lemon juice
3 to 4 ounces chilled soda water

FOR GARNISHING
Fresh strawberry
Small basil leaf

In a cocktail shaker, press the basil and strawberries together with a muddler to release the basil's flavor. Fill the shaker with ice. Measure in the vodka and lemon juice. Cap and shake vigorously. Pour into a large glass, top with soda water, and stir. Garnish with a strawberry and basil leaf.

Sugared Strawberries

MAKES ENOUGH FOR ABOUT 6 DRINKS

1 pint fresh strawberries, stemmed and thinly sliced
1½ cups powdered sugar

Mix the ingredients together in a small bowl and let sit for 15 minutes before using.

Lush

Modeled on the classic sidecar, Lush is kicked into a different gear with peach-flavored rum and brandy. The syrup injects just the right amount of spice and sweet to offset the fresh lemon. This drink can also be made with peach vodka instead of rum.

Spiced Sugar (recipe follows)
1 orange wedge
1½ ounces Bacardi Peach Red rum
½ ounce brandy
½ ounce fresh lemon juice
¾ ounce Honey Spice Syrup (facing page)

FOR GARNISHING
Long orange-zest twist

Rim a martini glass (see page 21) with the spiced sugar, and set aside.

Squeeze the orange wedge into a cocktail shaker and drop in. Fill the shaker with ice. Measure in the rum, brandy, lemon juice, and syrup. Cap and shake vigorously. Strain into the sugar-rimmed glass. Garnish with an orange twist.

Spiced Sugar

MAKES ½ CUP

½ cup superfine or baker's sugar
¼ teaspoon ground cloves
¼ teaspoon ground allspice

Mix the ingredients in a small bowl. Store in a tightly covered container at room temperature for up to 6 months. Shake or stir before using to remix the ingredients.

Honey Spice Syrup

MAKES 1 CUP, ENOUGH FOR ABOUT 10 DRINKS

$^1\!/_2$ cup honey

$^1\!/_4$ teaspoon ground cloves

$^1\!/_4$ teaspoon ground allspice

$^1\!/_4$ teaspoon ground nutmeg

$^1\!/_2$ cup boiling water

Combine the honey and spices in a heatproof glass jar. Add the boiling water and stir. Let cool to room temperature and sit for 2 days before using. It keeps, refrigerated, for up to 3 weeks.

Preso

MAKES 1 DRINK

For the person looking to push the boundaries of their drink repertoire, this Italian-inspired cocktail unites lightly muddled green grapes with fiery grappa, softened by Tuaca's citrus and vanilla notes. A tiny drop of olive oil adds a velvety mouthfeel.

6 green grapes

$1^1\!/_2$ ounces vodka

$^1\!/_8$ ounce grappa

$^1\!/_2$ ounce Tuaca

FOR GARNISHING

Green grape

1 drop very high-quality extra-virgin olive oil (optional)

In a cocktail shaker, press 6 grapes with a muddler to release the flavor. Fill the shaker with ice. Measure in the vodka, grappa, and Tuaca. Cap and shake vigorously. Strain into a martini glass. Drop in a grape and place 1 drop of olive oil, if using, in the center of the cocktail for garnish.

Ginger Sake Cocktail "Sushi"

These sophisticated little "hip sips" can be eaten in one bite, like sushi. They're super-fun to pass at a party along with appetizers. Just don't eat too many—they're quite potent!

3 ($\frac{1}{4}$-ounce) packets Knox unflavored gelatin

6 ounces sake

10 ounces Simple Syrup (page 19)

1 tablespoon very finely minced peeled fresh ginger

12 ounces vodka

6 ounces fresh lime juice

FOR GARNISHING

25 to 30 thin slices cucumber

Edible gold flakes (see page 199)

Tiny-julienne candied ginger (optional)

In a small bowl, sprinkle the gelatin over the sake and let soak for 5 minutes to bloom the gelatin.

In a small saucepan over medium-high heat, bring the simple syrup and ginger just to a boil. Remove from the heat. Add the gelatin and sake mixture, and stir to completely dissolve the gelatin. Stir in the vodka and lime juice.

Carefully pour the mixture into a plastic wrap–lined 8-inch-square glass baking dish. Cover tightly with plastic wrap, not touching the liquid surface, and refrigerate until the gelatin is completely set, preferably overnight.

To serve, unmold the gelatin onto a parchment- or wax paper–lined baking sheet. Remove the plastic wrap and cut gelatin into desired shapes. (I like to use a 1-inch round cutter or to cut the gelatin into squares.) Serve each piece on a slice of cucumber, and top with a tiny sprinkle of gold and/or ginger, if using.

Black Feather

Cocktail authority Robert Hess created this French-ingredient-inspired drink as his house cocktail. He started DrinkBoy.com to allow bartenders around the world to share ideas; it is one of the most visited cocktail sites on the Web.

2 ounces Cognac or high-quality brandy

1 ounce dry white vermouth

½ ounce Cointreau

1 dash Angostura bitters

FOR GARNISHING

Lemon-zest twist

Fill a cocktail shaker with ice. Measure in the Cognac, vermouth, and Cointreau. Add the bitters. Stir with a bar spoon for no less than 30 seconds, until the shaker is frosty. Strain into a martini glass. Garnish with a lemon twist.

Gin Flower Crush

The floral essence of elderflower liqueur blends with gin's layers of flavor for a multidimensional drink. If you live in an area with citrus trees, an unsprayed lemon or orange blossom would be a beautiful garnish.

2 ounces gin

¾ ounce St. Germain elderflower liqueur

1½ ounces Fresh Lemon Sour (page 20)

⅛ ounce fresh lemon juice

FOR GARNISHING

Long lemon-zest twist

Long orange-zest twist

Fill a cocktail shaker with ice. Measure in the gin, elderflower liqueur, lemon sour, and lemon juice. Cap and shake vigorously. Strain into a martini glass. Twist the citrus-zest pieces together, then lay them over and into the drink.

Cheladas

This refreshing Mexican drink dates back to the 1940s or '50s. The classic and new variations are making a popular splash on the U.S. bar scene. ¡Viva!

Classic Chelada

> Kosher salt or other coarse salt for rimming glass (optional)
>
> Juice of 1 medium lime (about ½ ounce juice)
>
> 1 (12-ounce) bottle Mexican beer, such as Negra Modelo or Corona
>
> FOR GARNISHING
>
> Lime wedge

Rim a tall or large glass (see page 21) with salt, and set aside.

Fill the glass with ice, add the lime juice, and top with beer. Garnish with a lime wedge. Serve any extra beer on the side.

Michelada

To the Classic Chelada recipe (above), add a dash of Worcestershire, hot sauce, or soy sauce to taste. Garnish with a pickled jalapeño and/or a fresh bell-pepper spear.

Roja Chelada

To the Classic Chelada recipe (top), add a dash of Worcestershire, hot sauce, or soy sauce to taste and 2 ounces of tomato juice or clamato juice. Garnish with red and yellow cherry tomatoes on a pick and/or a sprig of celery.

continued >

61

Fruta Chelada

Kosher salt or other coarse salt for rimming glass (optional)

2 tablespoons chopped fresh fruit, such as pineapple, mango, or melon

1 teaspoon sugar

Juice of 1 medium lime (about ½ ounce juice)

Dash of hot sauce (optional)

1 (12-ounce) bottle Pacifico beer

FOR GARNISHING

Fresh fruit wedge

Rim a tall or large glass (see page 21) with salt, and set aside.

In a cocktail shaker, press the chopped fruit and sugar together with a muddler to release the juice. Fill the shaker with ice and add the lime juice and hot sauce, if using. Stir and pour into the salt-rimmed glass. Top with beer. Garnish with fruit. Serve any extra beer on the side.

Cosmo Chi Chi

Combining two beloved drinks, the popular cosmo and the retro tropical chi chi, this is a super-fun girlfriend-party cocktail.

1½ ounces vodka

¼ ounce Grand Marnier

¾ ounce cranberry juice

1½ ounces Tropical Sweet & Sour (recipe follows)

FOR GARNISHING

1 fresh or frozen whole cranberry

Fill a cocktail shaker with ice. Measure in the vodka, Grand Marnier, cranberry juice, and sour. Cap and shake vigorously. Strain into a large martini glass. Float a whole cranberry for garnish.

Tropical Sweet & Sour

MAKES ABOUT 2 CUPS, OR ENOUGH FOR 10 COCKTAILS

½ cup Simple Syrup (page 19)

¼ cup fresh lime juice

¼ cup fresh lemon juice

¾ cup pineapple juice

3 tablespoons Coco Lopez sweetened cream of coconut

In a decorative bottle (because it looks nice when serving), shake the ingredients together. Refrigerate until ready to use. Shake well before each use. The mix can be stored, refrigerated, for up to 2 weeks.

Lill'pertif

This is my favorite aperitif cocktail. The aromatic and honey essence of Lillet plays well off the salty olive garnish. Accompany with Prosciutto Scallop Pops with Lemon Artichoke Pesto (page 174).

1½ ounces white Lillet

¾ ounce sweet red vermouth

¾ ounce vodka

FOR GARNISHING

Long lemon-zest twist

Green olive

Fill a rocks glass or large wine glass half full with ice. Add the Lillet, vermouth, and vodka. Stir. Twist the lemon zest directly over the glass, then drop in. Spear the olive on a pick and drop in.

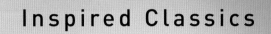
Inspired Classics

Ultra Martini Bar

I love to do a martini-bar party. I set out a selection of traditional and out-of-the-ordinary garnishes and shake up the martinis—then let guests embellish their own.

For an accompanying full-on appetizer spread, I recommend Sausage Olive Poppers (page 139), "Cocktail Shrimp" with Martini Aioli (page 186), and Mini Scallion Biscuits with Smoked Salmon Spread & Pickled Onions (page 156).

Classic Martini

⅛ ounce dry white vermouth

1½ ounces gin or vodka

FOR GARNISHING—SET OUT AN ASSORTMENT; HERE ARE A FEW IDEAS:

Assorted stuffed green olives, such as classic pimiento, blue cheese, garlic, and jalapeño

Long lemon-zest twists

Toasted-almond-stuffed olives

Giant caperberries with stems

Cornichons wrapped with thin slices of salami

Pickled cherry peppers or Spanish piparras peppers

Smoked salmon–wrapped pickled cocktail onions

Cubes of sexy cheese, such as smoked Gouda or a firm artisanal cheese

Tiny cubes of prosciutto-wrapped melon

Edible gold or silver flakes (see page 199)

Fill a small martini glass with ice and a splash of water to chill. Set aside.

Meanwhile, roll the vermouth around in a cocktail shaker, then shake out any excess. Fill the shaker with ice. Measure in the gin or vodka. Cap and shake—at least 15 times—until very cold.

Empty the ice from the martini glass. Strain the drink into the glass. Garnish as desired.

continued >

69

Some other martini variations to experiment with:

Vesper—2 parts gin, 1 part vodka, dash of Lillet

Gin Starter—1 part gin, 1 part vodka, wash of dry vermouth

Perfect Martini—2 parts gin, ½ part dry white vermouth, ½ part sweet red vermouth

Dirty Martini—Add a teaspoon of olive juice to a classic martini

Sake Martini—1 part vodka, dash of sake, garnish with cucumber or pickled ginger

Green-Eye Daiquiri

Daiquiris, which became all the rage in the 1940s, were a favorite of famed writer Ernest Hemingway. A jot of green Chartreuse, with its extracts of 130 plants, adds a sophisticated and unusual flavor. I think Papa would have approved.

2 sprigs fresh thyme

2 ounces white rum

1/8 ounce green Chartreuse

3/4 ounce fresh lime juice

1 1/2 teaspoons sugar

FOR GARNISHING

Fresh thyme sprig

Bend 2 thyme sprigs and drop into a cocktail shaker. Press the thyme with a muddler to release the flavor. Fill the shaker with ice. Measure in the rum, Chartreuse, lime juice, and sugar. Cap and shake vigorously. Strain into a martini glass. Garnish with a thyme sprig.

Peach 75

This cocktail is so summery. The anise scent of fresh tarragon plays well with peach in this revamped French 75. Croque Monsieur Puffs (page 194) add the right je ne sais quoi.

1 sprig fresh tarragon
1½ ounces Bombay Sapphire gin
¾ ounce fresh lemon juice
2 tablespoons Peach Puree (recipe follows)
¾ ounce Simple Syrup (page 19)
Splash of Champagne

FOR GARNISHING
Fresh tarragon sprig

Tear 1 tarragon sprig and drop into a cocktail shaker. Fill the shaker with ice. Measure in the gin, lemon juice, peach puree, and simple syrup. Cap and shake vigorously. Strain into a martini glass or Champagne flute. Top with a splash of Champagne. Garnish with a tarragon sprig.

Peach Puree

MAKES 1¾ CUPS, ENOUGH FOR ABOUT 12 TO 14 DRINKS

2 large fresh peaches, peeled and diced, or 2 cups frozen peach chunks, defrosted
1 tablespoon fresh lemon juice
1 tablespoon sugar

Combine the peaches, lemon juice, and sugar in a blender or food processor and process until smooth. If not using immediately, cover and refrigerate, for up to 2 days, until needed.

☞ TIP   You can also make this drink with 1 ounce of gin and 1 ounce of peach vodka, omitting the peach puree.

Montréal

Dubbed the Montréal by way of Canadian rye whisky and French Pernod, this urbane combination is pleasingly akin to a manhattan.

1½ ounces rye whisky

¾ ounce sweet red vermouth

⅛ ounce Pernod

3 dashes Peychaud's bitters

FOR GARNISHING

Long orange-zest twist

Fill a cocktail shaker with ice. Measure in the rye, vermouth, and Pernod. Add the bitters. Stir. Serve on the rocks in an old-fashioned glass, or strain into a martini glass. Garnish with an orange twist.

Dubious Manhattan

The spicy aroma of French Dubonnet Rouge ever so slightly modifies the traditional manhattan. My Drunken Plumped Cherries are a great alternative to maraschino cherries. This drink cries out for Bacon, Blue Cheese & Pecan Cocktail Cookies (page 143).

2 ounces bourbon

½ ounce Dubonnet Rouge

½ ounce sweet red vermouth

Dash of peach bitters

FOR GARNISHING

3 Drunken Plumped Cherries (page 76)

Fill a cocktail shaker with ice. Measure in the bourbon, Dubonnet, and vermouth. Add the bitters. Cap and shake vigorously. Strain into a martini glass. Spear the cherries on a pick and drop in.

Drunken Plumped Cherries

MAKES 1 CUP

½ cup dried sweet cherries
½ cup Dubonnet Rouge
¼ cup sugar
¼ cup hot water

Put cherries, Dubonnet, and sugar in a small bowl. Pour the hot water over the cherries and stir well. Cover and let sit at room temperature for at least 12 hours before using. Store, covered and refrigerated, for up to 2 months.

☛ TIP If you want to keep the flavor of the cherries more neutral for use in other drinks, substitute ¼ cup vodka for the Dubonnet and increase the sugar and water to ½ cup each.

Celery 'N' Tonic

MAKES 1 DRINK

The botanicals of gin along with the dry notes of celery and the slightly sweet-but-bitter tonic give this gin and tonic a fresh take. Served with Creole Crab "Cupcakes" (page 188) peppered with Old Bay, Celery 'N' Tonic is bound to be a front-porch classic.

2 tablespoons sliced celery
1½ ounces Bombay Sapphire gin
3 to 4 ounces chilled tonic water
2 dashes Peychaud's bitters

FOR GARNISHING
Small sprig of celery with leaves

In a cocktail shaker, crush the sliced celery with a muddler. Fill the shaker with ice. Measure in the gin. Cap and shake vigorously. Pour into a tall glass. Top with the tonic water and bitters, and stir. Garnish with a celery sprig.

Fresh Apple Mojito

Apple's sweet juiciness—along with the cooling character of mint—yields this exceptionally refreshing mojito. Choose local organic apples whenever possible. In summertime, exchange the apple for pitted fresh cherries. Shake up this drink to go with Bollywood Chicken Skewers with Spiced Yogurt Dip (page 140).

> 3 large sprigs fresh mint
> ¼ apple, cut into chunks
> 2 ounces white rum
> ¾ ounce fresh lime juice
> ¾ ounce Simple Syrup (page 19)
> Splash of chilled soda water

Tear the mint sprigs and drop into a cocktail shaker. Add the apple. With a muddler, press the mint and apple to release their flavors. Fill the shaker with ice. Measure in the rum, lime juice, and simple syrup. Cap and shake vigorously. Pour into a large glass. Top with soda water.

Poppy's Margarita

Spicy cocktails are hot! The counterbalance of sweet, sour, spice, and salt achieves a mouthwatering result. Put out bowls of Cha Cha Cashews (page 142) for a tasty nibble.

Kosher salt for rimming glass (optional)

Lime wedge

1 1/2 ounces Sauza gold tequila

1 1/2 ounces Spicy Chipotle-Lime Sour (recipe follows)

1/4 ounce triple sec or other orange-flavored liqueur (optional)

FOR GARNISHING

Lime wheel with a straw inserted through the middle (optional)

Rim an old-fashioned glass (see page 21) with kosher salt, and set aside.

Squeeze the lime wedge into a cocktail shaker and drop in. Fill the shaker with ice. Measure in the tequila, sour, and triple sec, if using. Cap and shake vigorously. Pour into an old-fashioned or tall glass. Garnish as desired.

Spicy Chipotle-Lime Sour

MAKES 3 CUPS, ENOUGH FOR ABOUT 16 DRINKS

1/4 teaspoon chipotle chile powder

1 cup sugar

1 cup water

1 1/2 cups fresh lime juice

In a small saucepan, combine the chile powder, sugar, and water and bring to a boil over high heat. Immediately remove from the heat and let cool to room temperature. Mix in the lime juice.

Transfer to a pretty bottle. Chill before using. The sour will keep for up to 2 weeks, refrigerated.

The Añejo Highball

MAKES 1 DRINK

This new classic was created by King of Cocktails Dale DeGroff. He is the founding president of the Museum of the American Cocktail. Dale's highball epitomizes a perfectly balanced cocktail—the richness of rum, tartness of citrus, sweetness of Curaçao, fizziness of ginger beer, and seasoning-like quality of bitters.

1½ ounces añejo rum
¾ ounce orange Curaçao
¼ ounce fresh lime juice
2 dashes Angostura bitters
2 ounces ginger beer

FOR GARNISHING
Lime wheel
Orange slice

Fill an old-fashioned or tall glass with ice. Measure in the rum, Curacao, and lime juice. Add the bitters and ginger beer. Garnish with a lime wheel and orange slice.

Ramos Passion Fizz

This ultimate brunch drink is "livelied up" with zingy passion-fruit nectar.

1 orange wedge
1$^1/_2$ ounces gin
$^1/_2$ ounce fresh lemon juice
1 ounce Looza passion-fruit nectar
$^1/_2$ ounce Simple Syrup (page 19)
$^1/_2$ ounce whipping cream
4 drops orange flower water
1 small egg white or 1 tablespoon pasteurized egg white
Splash of chilled soda water

FOR GARNISHING
Long orange-zest twist

Squeeze the orange wedge into a cocktail shaker and drop in. Measure in the gin, lemon juice, passion-fruit nectar, simple syrup, and whipping cream. Add the orange flower water and egg white. Fill the shaker with ice. Cap and shake vigorously for 10 seconds. Pour into a tall glass and top with a splash of soda water. Garnish with an orange twist.

Luxury Bloody Mary

If you love Bloody Marys, then it's worth it to make your own Mary mix. My version includes a little balsamic vinegar and celery seed. Homemade horseradish-infused vodka takes it over the top.

1½ ounces Horseradish-Infused Vodka (recipe follows),
    or substitute plain vodka
4 ounces Luxury Mary Mix (page 84)

FOR GARNISHING
Rosemary sprig
Lemon wedge
Garlic-stuffed olive

Fill a large old-fashioned or tall glass with ice. Measure in the infused vodka and Mary mix. Stir. Garnish with a rosemary sprig, lemon wedge, and an olive on a pick.

Horseradish-Infused Vodka

MAKES 3 CUPS, ENOUGH FOR ABOUT 16 DRINKS

1½ cups vodka
Three ¼-inch-thick slices peeled fresh horseradish

Combine the vodka and horseradish in a 4-cup glass jar. Cover and let infuse at room temperature for 24 hours. Strain the vodka, pressing out as much liquid from the horseradish as possible, and discard the horseradish. Store the infused vodka in a vodka bottle or other pretty bottle, tightly capped, for up to 6 months at room temperature.

Luxury Mary Mix

MAKES 7 CUPS, ENOUGH FOR ABOUT 14 DRINKS

1 (46-ounce) can tomato juice

¼ cup fresh lemon juice

¼ cup Worcestershire sauce

½ teaspoon freshly ground or coarse black pepper

6 tablespoons balsamic vinegar

1 tablespoon prepared horseradish

1 tablespoon hot pepper sauce

½ teaspoon celery seed (optional)

1 teaspoon salt

In a large glass or plastic pitcher, mix ingredients; make sure the salt dissolves. Cover and refrigerate, for up to 7 days.

Grapefruit Negroni

I had my first negroni while sitting in a piazza in Florence and have been hooked ever since. I add fresh grapefruit to my rendition. On a warm evening, serve these alfresco along with Olive Tapenade (page 153), Creamy White Bean Dip with Garlic & Rosemary (page 163), and Sassy Sherry-Roasted Peppers (page 164), all escorted by Herbed Crostini (page 198). Pair these antipasti, as well, with Tuscan Rosemary Lemon Drops (page 47) for a hint of la dolce vita.

¼ large red grapefruit

1½ ounces gin

¾ ounce sweet red vermouth

½ ounce Campari

FOR GARNISHING
Small grapefruit wedge

Squeeze the grapefruit into a cocktail shaker and discard the squeezed fruit. Fill the shaker with ice. Measure in the gin, vermouth, and Campari. Cap and shake vigorously. Strain into a martini glass or an old-fashioned glass filled with fresh ice. Garnish with a small grapefruit wedge.

Bistro Sidecar

I "stretched the sidecar theme to the max," according to spirits expert and author Gary Regan, when I created this cocktail in 2000. This new classic is now seen on cocktail menus across the United States.

Superfine sugar for rimming glass (optional)
1½ ounces brandy or Cognac
½ ounce Tuaca
½ ounce Frangelico
¼ ounce fresh lemon juice
½ ounce fresh tangerine or orange juice

FOR GARNISHING
Toasted hazelnut, with skin

Rim a martini glass (see page 21) with superfine sugar, and set aside.

Fill a cocktail shaker with ice. Measure in the brandy, liqueurs, and juices. Cap and shake vigorously. Strain into the sugar-rimmed glass. Float a toasted hazelnut on top of the drink.

Rusty Martini

A smoky martini gets "rusty" with a kiss of Drambuie.

Dash of Scotch
2 ounces vodka
¼ ounce Drambuie

FOR GARNISHING
Long orange-zest twist

Roll the Scotch around in a cocktail shaker, then shake out any excess. Fill the shaker with ice. Measure in the vodka and Drambuie. Cap and shake vigorously. Strain into a martini glass. Garnish with an orange twist.

English Old Fashioned

I have taken quite a lot of liberty here with the Old Fashioned, introducing a bit of Britain by incorporating Pimm's and its sidekick, the cucumber.

1 thin slice cucumber
1 orange wedge
1 maraschino cherry
1½ ounces bourbon
½ ounce Pimm's No. 1
1 dash Angostura bitters

In an old-fashioned glass, press the cucumber slice, orange wedge, and cherry with a muddler to release their flavors. Fill the glass to the top with ice. Measure in the bourbon and Pimm's. Add the bitters. Stir.

Pineapple Pisco Sour

The classic South American drink is lightened up here with pineapple juice. The sour gets its fluffy head from vigorously shaking in an egg white.

1½ ounces pisco
¾ ounce fresh lemon juice
¾ ounce pineapple juice
½ ounce Simple Syrup (page 19)
1 small egg white or 1 tablespoon pasteurized egg white

FOR GARNISHING
3 drops Angostura bitters

Fill a cocktail shaker with ice. Measure in the pisco, juices, and simple syrup. Add the egg white. Cap and shake vigorously for 10 seconds. Immediately strain into a very large martini glass. To garnish the drink, place 3 drops of bitters, spaced apart, on the foam. Pull the point of a cocktail pick or small knife through the bitters to make an abstract drawing.

Fresh Raspberry Bellini

Made with fresh raspberry puree, the color of this cocktail is strikingly beautiful. Serve at your next brunch or for a leisurely breakfast in bed! Also lovely as an aperitif on a lazy afternoon.

1 tablespoon Raspberry Puree (recipe follows)

½ ounce peach schnapps

4 to 5 ounces chilled Prosecco or brut or dry rose Champagne

FOR GARNISHING

Fresh raspberry

Place the puree in the bottom of a slender tall glass or champagne flute. Add the schnapps, then the Prosecco. Stir with a bar spoon. Garnish with a raspberry.

Raspberry Puree

MAKES 1 CUP, ENOUGH FOR ABOUT 16 DRINKS

1 pint fresh raspberries or 2 cups frozen unsweetened raspberries, defrosted

1 tablespoon fresh lemon juice

1 tablespoon sugar

Combine the raspberries, lemon juice, and sugar in a blender or food processor and process until smooth. Strain through a fine sieve. If not using immediately, cover and refrigerate, for up to 4 days, until needed.

☛ TIP   If you would like a sweeter drink, add more sugar to the puree.

Mango Mai Tai

Mango rum adds a fantastic flavor punch to this already tasty tropical cocktail. Serve with crowd-pleasing Pineapple Avocado Salsa (page 146) and tortilla chips.

³⁄₄ ounce mango-flavored rum

³⁄₄ ounce dark rum

¹⁄₂ ounce amaretto, or substitute orgeat syrup

³⁄₄ ounce fresh lime juice

1 ounce pineapple juice

FOR GARNISHING

Paper parasol

Orange wedge

Fill an old-fashioned glass with ice. Measure in the rums, amaretto, and juices. Stir. Garnish with a parasol and orange wedge.

Sunshine Sour

Known as the Modern Mixologist, Tony Abou-Ganim is a leader in creative cocktails and has been a cocktail competitor on Iron Chef. *Tony's sour recipe typifies his style and his dedication to continually improving the art of the cocktail.*

1½ ounces Finlandia grapefruit vodka
½ ounce Aperol
1 ounce fresh lemon juice
1 ounce fresh orange juice
½ ounce Clover Honey Syrup (recipe follows)
1 small egg white or 1 tablespoon pasteurized egg whites (optional, but gives the drink a rich, creamy, frothy head)

FOR GARNISHING
Orange slice
Long lemon-zest twist

Fill a cocktail shaker with ice. Measure in the vodka, Aperol, juices, and syrup. Add the egg white, if using. Cap and shake vigorously. Strain into an old-fashioned glass filled with fresh ice. Garnish with an orange slice and a lemon twist.

Clover Honey Syrup

MAKES 1 CUP

½ cup clover honey
½ cup warm water

Combine honey and water and stir to mix. Cover and refrigerate, for up to 2 weeks, until needed.

Rocapulco Red

The classic tequila sunrise gets updated by trading out super-sweet traditional grenadine syrup for tangy drier pomegranate juice—a delicious way to get your antioxidant boost. When fresh pomegranates are in season, sprinkle some seeds on top of the drink.

1 lime wedge

1½ ounces Cazadores reposado tequila

3 ounces fresh orange juice

1½ ounces pomegranate juice

Squeeze the lime wedge into a tall glass and drop in. Fill the glass with ice. Measure in the tequila and orange juice. Stir. Drizzle the pomegranate juice over the top. The juice will drip down into the drink for a striking presentation.

Cocktails for a Crowd

Summer Melon Sangria

MAKES ABOUT 4 CUPS
(6 TO 8 SERVINGS)

Tall cool glasses of this peak-of-summer sangria are smashing with Greek Salsa with Pita Crisps (page 160). Try using other juicy ripe melons, such as honeydew and/or casaba. You can make this drink up to two days before serving.

1 (750 ml) bottle dry white wine, such as dry Riesling

3 tablespoons Midori melon liqueur

1 lime, thinly sliced

2 kiwifruit, peeled and sliced

2 cups peeled, seeded, and cubed watermelon

1/4 cup sugar

In a large pitcher, combine all the ingredients and stir with a spoon, crushing some of the fruit. Cover and refrigerate overnight or for at least 12 hours to let the flavors marry before serving. Serve over ice, and include some of the fruit in each serving.

Berrylicious Sangria

MAKES ABOUT 4 CUPS
(6 TO 8 SERVINGS)

Fresh berries mingle with red wine for a festive patio-party libation. Experiment with a variety of berries, such as sliced strawberries, raspberries, and blackberries.

1 (750 ml) bottle red wine, preferably dry

2 tablespoons brandy

1 1/2 cups mixed fresh berries

1/2 lemon, cut into thin slices

6 tablespoons sugar or 1/4 cup honey

In a large pitcher, combine all the ingredients and stir gently to mix. Cover and refrigerate for at least 4 hours or up to 2 days. When ready to serve, pour into large wine glasses or fun tall glasses and include a little of the fruit in each serving.

Cheaters Blended Margarita

Years ago, a friend made me a margarita using limeade concentrate, tequila, and beer . . . and it was crazy good! So, I've made up my own concoction here. What the heck, we're all too busy sometimes! If you want to keep it on the down low, premix it (then hide the cans!) and put it in a pitcher, ready for blending. To use up that extra time you have from cheating on the drink, consider making Lamb "Sliders" on Homemade Rosemary Buns (page 148) . . . yummy!

¾ cup Sauza gold tequila

¼ cup triple sec

1 (6-ounce) can frozen limeade concentrate, defrosted

½ (12-ounce) bottle mild-flavored or light beer

4 cups ice

FOR GARNISHING
Lime wheels

Measure the drink ingredients into a large blender jar. Blend until smooth. Serve in margarita or old-fashioned glasses. Garnish with lime wheels.

FOR FUN VARIATIONS, TRY BLENDING IN ONE OF THE FOLLOWING:

½ cup cranberry juice

½ cup pomegranate juice

½ cup blueberry juice

¾ cup sliced fresh strawberries

¾ cup cubed fresh mango

☛ TIP If you have a small blender, then process half batches. Serve in kosher salt–rimmed glasses (see page 21), if desired. Sometimes I like to do "half-salted" rims.

Sake Sangria

In crafting this drink, I tried several different brands of sake and found that an inexpensive dry sake definitely works. Accompany with Coriander Citrus Shrimp "Lollipops" (page 145) and Sake Teriyaki Sticky Chicken Wings (page 178). Kampai!

1 (750 ml) bottle sake

6 tablespoons honey

2-inch piece of fresh ginger, peeled and thinly sliced

1 stalk fresh lemongrass, halved lengthwise, then cut into 3- to 4-inch pieces (use the entire stalk)

½ lemon, thinly sliced

1 small tangerine or orange, thinly sliced

1 large plum or apricot, pitted and cut into thin wedges (optional, if not in season)

In a large pitcher, combine all the ingredients and stir with a spoon, crushing some of the fruit. Cover and refrigerate for at least 12 hours, or up to 2 days, to let the flavors marry before serving. Serve over ice, and include some of the fruit in each serving.

Lilikoi Rum Punch

Lilikoi is the yellow passion fruit, slightly larger and tarter than the purple variety. In this punch for a crowd, I use a widely available bottled passion-fruit nectar. Perfect to serve at any tropical- or tiki-themed party.

1 (750 ml) bottle spiced rum
3 cups Looza passion-fruit nectar
1 cup fresh lime juice
2 cups pineapple juice
Chilled soda water (optional)

FOR GARNISHING
Lime wedges, edible flowers, or paper parasols

In a large pitcher, combine the rum, passion-fruit nectar, and juices. Stir. If not serving immediately, cover and refrigerate, for up to 4 days, until needed.

To serve, fill old-fashioned or tall glasses with ice and pour in the rum punch. I like to add a little splash of soda water to lighten the drink a bit. Garnish as desired.

Hibiscus Rum Punch

Start the party! Tall glasses of this thirst-quenching iced punch are so pretty—its hot pink, all-natural color comes from brilliant dried hibiscus flowers steeped like tea. You can find them in the bulk foods or tea sections at natural foods grocers, as well as at Mexican grocers, where hibiscus is called jamaica—*yes, it's the Caribbean island's name!*

6 cups boiling water

½ cup dried hibiscus flowers

1 cup honey

2 cups white or spiced rum

1 cup fresh lime juice

½ teaspoon Angostura bitters (optional)

FOR GARNISHING

Lime wheels or edible flowers

In a medium nonreactive saucepan, bring the water to a boil and add the hibiscus flowers. Remove from the heat and let steep for 10 minutes. Strain the hibiscus tea into a large heatproof container or pitcher and discard the solids. Stir in the honey. Place in refrigerator to chill. When mixture is cold, stir in the rum, lime juice, and bitters, if using. The punch keeps, covered and refrigerated, for up to 4 days.

To serve, fill tall or old-fashioned glasses to the top with ice. Pour in about ¾ cup (6 fluid ounces) of punch. Garnish as desired.

103

Bliss Wedding Punch

This recipe can be doubled, tripled, or more, depending upon how many guests you are expecting. If fresh strawberries are out of season, you can always make the punch with unsweetened frozen berries and garnish with fresh mint sprigs or edible flowers. When serving a punch, add ice to individual glasses rather than to the punch bowl, to avoid diluting the punch.

½ (15-ounce) can Coco Lopez sweetened cream of coconut
1½ cups fresh lime juice
1½ cups fresh lemon juice
1 (46-ounce) can pineapple juice
3 cups cranberry juice
2 (750 ml) bottles vodka
2 cups Simple Syrup (page 19)
1 pint fresh strawberries, stemmed and pureed
1 liter (about 4 cups) chilled soda water

FOR GARNISHING
Fresh strawberries

105

In a large container that will hold at least 1½ gallons, whisk the Coco Lopez with a little of the lime juice until smooth; this will thin out the Coco Lopez. Add the remaining lime juice; lemon, pineapple, and cranberry juices; vodka; simple syrup; and strawberry puree. Whisk until thoroughly combined. Transfer to clean plastic jugs or bottles and refrigerate until needed, for up to 1 week.

When ready to serve, shake the bottles to remix the ingredients and then pour the mixture into a large punch bowl. Stir in the soda water. Serve in ice-filled glasses and garnish with strawberries.

Cosmo Cooler for a Crowd

My big-batch recipe for this much-loved sexy cocktail gets a flavor-smoothing and a nice effervescence from the addition of light beer.

1 (750 ml) bottle vodka

1½ cups fresh lime juice

1½ cups cranberry juice

1½ cups Simple Syrup (page 19)

2 (12-ounce) bottles Corona Light, chilled

FOR GARNISHING

Fresh or frozen cranberries and/or lime wedges

In a large nonreactive container, such as a glass pitcher, combine the vodka, juices, and simple syrup. Right before serving, stir in the beer.

Serve over ice in old-fashioned glasses or tumblers. Garnish as desired.

Spiked Southern Iced Tea Punch

Tea-based punches are oh-so-Southern and evoke lazy days on the veranda. For a more-spiked interpretation, let guests add a little more whiskey to their individual drinks.

20 whole cloves

1 orange

6 very large sprigs fresh mint

3 tea bags black tea

3 cups boiling water

1 cup ice water

1 cup fresh orange juice

$\frac{1}{2}$ cup fresh lemon juice

1 cup pineapple juice

$\frac{1}{2}$ cup packed brown sugar

1$\frac{1}{2}$ cups Jack Daniel's whiskey or bourbon

FOR GARNISHING

Fresh or frozen cranberries and/or lime wedges

Poke the cloves into the orange, then cut it into 3 slices. Put the orange slices, mint, and tea bags in a heatproof pitcher or bowl. Add the boiling water, let steep for 1 hour, then remove the tea bags.

Add the ice water, juices, and brown sugar. Stir until the sugar is dissolved, then chill until ready to serve. Stir in the whiskey and serve in ice-filled glasses. Garnish as desired.

Clear-Headed Cocktails

Blackberry Lemonade

For a delicious variation, toss in a pinch of dried lavender or a couple of flowering sprigs of fresh lavender when you cook the syrup. This 'ade's also fabulous with some gin or vodka added.

2 ounces Blackberry-Lemon Syrup (recipe follows)
4 ounces chilled soda water

FOR GARNISHING
Lemon wheel
Fresh blackberries

Fill a tall glass with ice. Measure in the syrup and soda water. Stir. Garnish with a lemon wheel and a few fresh blackberries.

Blackberry-Lemon Syrup

MAKES 1½ CUPS, ENOUGH FOR ABOUT 6 SERVINGS

1 cup water
½ cup sugar
½ cup fresh blackberries, or substitute frozen
1 tablespoon thinly sliced lemon zest (see Tip)
1 cup fresh lemon juice

Combine the ingredients in a small heavy saucepan. Bring to a boil over high heat, and boil for 2 minutes. Remove from the heat. Strain through a very fine strainer, pressing out as much liquid as possible. Discard the solids and let the syrup cool to room temperature. If not using immediately, cover and refrigerate, for up to 7 days, until needed.

☛ TIP   With a potato peeler, cut off only the yellow part of the lemon skin. Peel it off in long strips, then cut the strips into thin slivers (julienne).

Clear Conscience

I created this drink for restaurateur friends who wanted a sophisticated drier non-alcoholic drink. Fresh lemon verbena can be hard to find, so if you have a spot on your deck or in your garden, I urge you to plant this aromatically fantastic herb. Once you get acquainted, you'll find many uses for it. I pick and freeze the leaves in late summer for wintertime use. If lemon verbena is unavailable, you can substitute lemon thyme, lemon balm, or a kaffir lime leaf.

¼ large tangerine or 1 large orange wedge

6 thin slices cucumber

1 fresh lemon verbena leaf

3 ounces Fresh Lemon-Lime Sour (page 20)

2 ounces chilled soda water

FOR GARNISHING

Sprig of fresh lemon verbena and/or paper-thin slice of cucumber

Squeeze the tangerine into a cocktail shaker and drop in. Add the cucumber and lemon verbena and press with a muddler to release their flavors. Fill the shaker with ice. Measure in the sour. Cap and shake vigorously. Add the soda, then strain into a large martini glass. Garnish as desired.

Cucumber Elderflower Fizz

Elderflower is much more these days than your great-grandmother's homemade wine. Tasting a lot like honeysuckle, this floral sweet syrup teams nicely with the cool green character of fresh cucumber and citrus for a hip sipper.

5 slices cucumber

1 ounce Fresh Lemon-Lime Sour (page 20)

$\frac{1}{2}$ ounce elderflower syrup, such as Monin (see page 199)

3 to 3½ ounces chilled soda water

FOR GARNISHING

Tiny sprig of Douglas fir

Fresh or frozen cranberry

In a cocktail shaker, press the cucumber slices with a muddler to release the flavor. Fill the shaker with ice. Measure in the sour and elderflower syrup. Cap and shake vigorously. Pour into a tall glass, add the soda water, and stir. Garnish as desired, and serve with a long, fat straw.

Pomarose

Fresh rosemary and grapefruit temper the sweetness of the sparkling cider. This excellent all-occasion cocktail can go both ways: add a shot of vodka for those who wish to imbibe.

1 sprig fresh rosemary
1 large red grapefruit wedge
1½ ounces pomegranate juice
3 ounces sparkling apple cider

FOR GARNISHING
Fresh rosemary sprig and/or thin slice of green apple

Bend the rosemary sprig and drop into a cocktail shaker. Squeeze in the grapefruit and drop in. Fill the shaker with ice. Measure in the pomegranate juice. Cap and shake vigorously. Pour into a tall glass. Top with the cider. Garnish as desired.

Cherry-Almond Spritzer

The classic combo of cherry and almond comes together again in this tasty spritzer.
If fresh cherries are out of season, substitute frozen unsweetened dark cherries.

2 ounces Cherry-Almond Syrup (recipe follows)

4 ounces soda water

FOR GARNISHING

Fresh cherry with stem, long lemon-zest twist, or toasted sliced almonds

Fill a tall glass with ice. Measure in the syrup and soda water. Stir. Garnish as desired.

Cherry-Almond Syrup

MAKES 1 3/4 CUPS, ENOUGH FOR ABOUT 7 SERVINGS

2 cups fresh sweet cherries, pitted

1/2 cup (1 1/2 to 1 3/4 ounces) sliced almonds, with skins

1 1/2 cups water

1 cup sugar

1/4 cup fresh lemon juice

1/2 teaspoon almond extract

In a small heavy saucepan, combine the cherries, almonds, water, and sugar. Bring to a boil over high heat and boil for 5 minutes. Remove from the heat and let cool. Transfer the cooked mixture to a blender, add the lemon juice and almond extract, and blend until coarsely chopped. Strain through a very fine strainer, pressing out as much liquid as possible, then discard the solids. If not using immediately, cover and refrigerate, for up to 7 days, until needed.

Herbalicious H2O

The name says it all! Clean and fresh, this drink has no sugar and is very spa-like with its infusion of botanicals.

6 large sprigs fresh mint

4 large sprigs fresh cilantro

1 small lemon, cut into thin slices

1 tangerine, cut into thin slices

4 thin slices peeled fresh ginger

6 cups water

FOR GARNISHING

Fresh cilantro or mint sprigs

Tear the 6 mint and 4 cilantro sprigs and drop into a medium container. Add the fruit, ginger, and water and stir. Cover and refrigerate, overnight, to infuse before using.

Serve over ice, in large wine glasses with some of the fruit in each serving. Garnish as desired.

117

Liquid Desserts
& Hot Drinks

Lemon Meringue Puff

Lemon meringue pie has always been my favorite, and I've had a vision of this drink for years. The liquid part mimics the tart-and-tangy pie filling. Then it just had to have a puffy meringue top! Baked till crisp, the puff floats on the drink and completes the "full pie experience" when nibbled with a sip.

1½ ounces citrus vodka

½ ounce Tuaca

¾ ounce fresh lemon juice

½ ounce Simple Syrup (page 19)

FOR GARNISHING

1 Meringue Puff (page 122)

Finely grated lemon zest

Yellow edible glitter (optional) (see page 199)

Fill a cocktail shaker with ice. Measure in the vodka, Tuaca, lemon juice, and simple syrup. Cap and shake vigorously. Strain into a martini glass. Float a meringue puff on top. With a microplane or other fine grater, grate a little lemon zest over the top, then sprinkle with glitter, if using. Serve immediately.

Meringue Puffs

MAKES ABOUT 20 PUFFS

¼ cup granulated sugar

¼ cup powdered sugar

2 large or 3 small egg whites, free of any egg yolk

1 teaspoon fresh lemon juice

1 tablespoon very finely minced lemon zest

Preheat an oven to 250 degrees F.

Mix the sugars in a small bowl, and set aside. In a grease-free (not plastic) mixer bowl, whip the egg whites with an electric mixer with a whip attachment on medium-high speed for about 2 minutes. Add the lemon juice and, with the mixer running, gradually add the sugar mixture. When all the sugar is incorporated, stop and scrape down the sides of the bowl, then continue whipping the meringue until stiff peaks are formed. Stir in the lemon zest. Total whipping time should be about 4½ minutes.

Transfer the meringue to a pastry bag fitted with a large star tip. Line a baking sheet with parchment paper or aluminum foil. Pipe the meringue into swirls, 1½ to 2 inches in diameter, and spaced at least 1 inch apart.

Bake the meringues for 40 minutes, then turn off heat and leave them in the oven until they are very dry, an additional hour or up to overnight.

Very carefully remove the meringues from the parchment paper, pulling back the paper or using a metal spatula. When the meringues are completely cooled, store in an airtight container for up to 3 days, depending on how moist your climate is.

'Fogato Chill

Affogato, meaning "drowned" in Italian, refers to ice cream in hot espresso. In my cocktail version, ice cream is drowned with chilled coffee liqueur and vodka, making for a bene little something after dinner.

1 ounce Starbucks coffee liqueur

1 ounce vodka

1 heaping tablespoon high-quality vanilla ice cream,
   scooped into an oval shape

FOR GARNISHING
Whole coffee bean

Fill a cocktail shaker with ice. Measure in the liqueur and vodka. Cap and shake vigorously. Strain into a martini glass. Float the ice cream in the drink, drop in a coffee bean for garnish, and serve immediately.

LIQUID DESSERTS & HOT DRINKS

Berry Orange Creamsicle

Here I've given an adult spin to a childhood treat with a flourish of luxurious berry liqueur.

¾ ounce Chambord
¾ ounce triple sec
1 ounce fresh orange juice
1 ounce whipping cream
1 ounce chilled soda water

FOR GARNISHING
Fresh raspberry if in season and/or long orange-zest twist

Fill a cocktail shaker with ice. Measure in the Chambord, triple sec, orange juice, and whipping cream. Cap and shake vigorously. Strain into a martini glass. Top with soda water. Garnish as desired.

Coconut Cake Colada Shot

This liquid dessert could be considered dangerous . . . as it goes down easy!

1 ounce Malibu coconut-flavored rum

1 ounce vanilla vodka

1 ounce pineapple juice

FOR GARNISHING

Maraschino cherry with stem

Fill a cocktail shaker with ice. Measure in the rum, vodka, and pineapple juice. Cap and shake vigorously. Strain into a sexy tall shot glass. Garnish with a maraschino cherry.

Mayan Hot Chocolate

Hot chocolate is the ideal vehicle not only for warm fragrant cinnamon, but also for pungent spices such as smoky chipotle chile and coriander. You can make up the cocoa mix to keep around for a quick after-dinner chocolate fix.

About 3 tablespoons Mayan Chocolate Mix (recipe follows),
  depending on how chocolaty you like your cocoa

$^3/_4$ cup hot milk

$^3/_4$ ounce brandy

$^1/_2$ ounce amaretto

FOR GARNISHING
Sweetened whipped cream or big marshmallows
Ground cinnamon

Put the chocolate mix in a mug, glass coffee cup, or tempered glass and stir in the hot milk, mixing well. Stir in the brandy and amaretto. Garnish with a dollop of whipped cream or a marshmallow and sprinkle with cinnamon.

Mayan Chocolate Mix

MAKES 2 $^3/_4$ CUPS, ENOUGH FOR ABOUT 12 TO 14 SERVINGS

$1^1/_2$ cups superfine or baker's sugar

$^1/_4$ cup packed brown sugar

1 teaspoon vanilla extract

$^3/_4$ cup unsweetened cocoa powder

$1^1/_2$ teaspoons ground cinnamon

$^1/_2$ teaspoon chipotle chile powder

$^3/_4$ teaspoon ground coriander

In a medium bowl, whisk together the sugars and vanilla extract. Add the remaining ingredients and whisk thoroughly to evenly distribute the cocoa and spices. Store at room temperature for up to 2 months, in a clean glass jar with a tight lid. Shake thoroughly before using to remix the ingredients.

Royal Coffee with Brown-Sugar Cream

I adore Amarula Cream liqueur, which is made from the South African marula fruit, a relative of the mango. This cocktail is a luxurious dessert alternative, especially when offered up with a simple chocolate truffle. Be sure your coffee is extra-hot and robust!

1 ounce Amarula Cream liqueur

¾ ounce Buttershots butterscotch schnapps

4 to 5 ounces hot coffee

2 tablespoons Brown-Sugar Cream (recipe follows)

In a coffee mug, cup, or heat-proof glass, combine the Amarula, Buttershots, and coffee. Stir gently. Dollop with the brown-sugar cream and serve immediately.

Brown-Sugar Cream

MAKES ABOUT ¾ CUP, ENOUGH FOR 6 DRINKS

½ cup whipping cream

2 tablespoons packed brown sugar

Make just before using. Combine the ingredients in a chilled mixing bowl and whip until soft peaks form.

Holiday Hot-Buttered Rum

Leave the grocery-store hot buttered rum out for Santa, and keep this for yourself! Ice cream adds a frothy richness to this winter warmer. Try it, also, with spiced rum, or omit the rum, and mix it with hot coffee for a cheery nonalcoholic drink.

1 to 1½ ounces rum

3 tablespoons Holiday Hot-Buttered Rum Mix (recipe follows)

½ cup boiling water

Measure the rum and hot buttered rum mix into a coffee mug, cup, or heatproof glass, then add the boiling water. Stir until evenly mixed.

Holiday Hot-Buttered Rum Mix

MAKES 2 CUPS, ENOUGH FOR ABOUT 10 DRINKS

8 tablespoons (1 stick) salted butter at room temperature

¾ cup packed brown sugar

¾ cup powdered sugar

1½ teaspoons very finely minced orange zest

1½ teaspoons very finely minced lemon zest

¾ teaspoon ground nutmeg

⅛ teaspoon ground cloves

¾ teaspoon ground cinnamon

⅛ teaspoon ground allspice

1 cup (½ pint) vanilla ice cream, softened

1½ teaspoons vanilla extract

In a mixing bowl, whip the butter, sugars, citrus zests, and spices with an electric mixer on high speed for about 5 minutes, until fluffy. Stop and scrape the bottom and sides of the bowl with a spatula. Add the ice cream and vanilla extract and whip on medium-high for 1½ minutes. Stop and scrape the bowl again, then whip on high for about 1 minute more, or until smooth. If the mixture looks broken, keep whipping; it will come together. The mix keeps, refrigerated, for up to one week, or, frozen, for up to 2 months. If frozen, defrost before using.

Warm Spiced White Wine

For large parties, this recipe can easily be increased, made in advance, and then gently reheated before serving. Keep it warm in a slow-cooker on low heat or in a deep, pretty chaffing dish. If you are a die-hard fan of spiced red wine, you can substitute it here.

12 whole cloves

1 small red apple, such as Pink Lady or Fuji

1 small ripe pear

5 allspice berries

1 cinnamon stick, broken in half

$\frac{1}{3}$ cup packed brown sugar

2 (750 ml) bottles light, dry white wine, such as chenin blanc

$\frac{1}{2}$ cup Grand Marnier or Cointreau

FOR GARNISHING

Orange-zest twists

Poke the cloves into the apple, then cut it into 5 slices. Cut the pear into 6 slices. Combine the fruit and remaining ingredients in a stainless-steel or heatproof glass pan and stir well to incorporate the brown sugar. Warm the mixture over low heat. Do not let it boil! Let the flavors steep for at least 30 minutes before serving. Serve warm in mugs, glass coffee cups, or tempered glasses. Garnish each serving with an orange twist.

Harvest Pumpkin Toddy

This should be a first-choice to serve at your next Halloween jack-o'-lantern carving party, Thanksgiving get-together, or fall celebration dinner.

1 lemon wedge

1 ounce brandy or bourbon

½ ounce Frangelico (optional)

2 tablespoons Spiced Pumpkin Mix (recipe follows)

½ cup boiling water

FOR GARNISHING

Cinnamon stick (optional)

Squeeze the lemon wedge into a coffee mug, cup, or heatproof glass, then drop in the rind. Measure in the brandy, Frangelico, if using, and pumpkin mix, then add the boiling water. Stir until evenly mixed. Garnish with a cinnamon stick, if using.

Spiced Pumpkin Mix

MAKES 3 CUPS, ENOUGH FOR 24 DRINKS

8 tablespoons (1 stick) salted butter at room temperature

1½ cups packed brown sugar

1 tablespoon ground cinnamon

2 teaspoons ground nutmeg

¾ teaspoon ground cloves

1 (15-ounce) can pumpkin puree

In a mixing bowl, whip the butter, brown sugar, and spices with an electric mixer on high speed for about 2 minutes, until light and fluffy. Stop and scrape the bowl as needed. Add the pumpkin and continue to whip until pumpkin is totally incorporated and mixture is fluffy, about 5 minutes more. If not using immediately, cover and refrigerate for up to 1 week or freeze for up to 2 months.

Minty Mocha

A chocolate lover's delight! Try making in mini form to serve as part of a chocolate dessert sampler.

3 sprigs fresh mint

1 ounce Starbucks coffee liqueur

$1/2$ ounce white crème de menthe or peppermint schnapps

1 ounce bourbon

2 tablespoons chocolate sauce

3 ounces whole milk

FOR GARNISHING

Whipped cream

Chocolate shavings

Fresh mint sprig

Bend the 3 mint sprigs and drop into a cocktail shaker. Fill the shaker with ice. Measure in the liqueurs, bourbon, chocolate sauce, and milk. Cap and shake vigorously. Strain the drink into a large glass filled with fresh ice. Garnish with a pouf of whipped cream, a few chocolate shavings, and mint.

☛ TIP   This drink can be made with vodka or brandy instead of bourbon, if you prefer.

Key Lime Pie

For a "Wow!" presentation, you can rim the glass with graham-cracker crumbs. Put a shallow pool of simple syrup on a small plate and spread a shallow layer of finely crushed crumbs on another small plate. Dip the rim of a large martini glass in the simple syrup, and then into the crumbs. Set aside while you make the drink.

2 ounces vanilla vodka

3/4 ounce fresh lime juice

1 ounce pineapple juice

1/2 ounce Simple Syrup (page 19)

1/2 ounce whipping cream

FOR GARNISHING

Thin lime wheel

Fill a cocktail shaker with ice. Measure in the vodka, juices, simple syrup, and whipping cream. Cap and shake vigorously. Strain into a martini glass. Float a lime wheel in the drink for garnish.

Blueberry'cello

*This homemade berry-infused limoncello is sweet to serve after dinner in small
cordial glasses or on the rocks. For a spritzer, serve the liqueur on the rocks with
a splash of chilled soda water, a squeeze of fresh lemon, and a lemon twist.*

1 1/2 cups fresh blueberries
1 (750 ml) bottle vodka
1 lemon
1 1/2 cups sugar
1 cup water

Put the berries in a bowl and mash with a potato masher or lightly crush with
clean hands to break them up. Divide the berries and vodka between two clean
4-cup glass jars with lids.

With a potato peeler, peel the zest from the lemon, being sure not to get any white
pith. Divide the zest between the jars. (Use the rest of the lemon for another
purpose.)

Cap the jars and shake well. Let sit at room temperature for 1 week, shaking the
jars every couple of days.

After 1 week, bring the sugar and water to a boil in a large saucepan, stirring to
dissolve the sugar. Boil for 2 minutes, then let cool to room temperature.

Using a coffee filter fitted into a strainer, strain the vodka into a big bowl to catch
every drop! (Be sure to press out all the liquid you can from the berries before you
discard them.)

Stir the cooled sugar syrup into the strained liquor. At this point, you can bottle
your Blueberry'cello into fancy bottles or clean clear wine bottles. Cap tightly and
store, at room temperature, for up to 2 months or, refrigerated, for 1 year.

Appetizers

continued >

Sausage Olive Poppers

Salty spicy sausage surrounds a pimiento-stuffed olive before it's rolled in bread crumbs and baked. You must have a cocktail with these . . . yum!

28 medium-sized pimiento-stuffed green olives
½ cup Italian-style bread crumbs
1 pound medium or hot Italian sausage, bulk or removed from casings

Spray a rimmed baking sheet with cooking spray, or lightly oil it, and set aside. Drain the olives well and dry on paper towels. Put the crumbs in a shallow bowl.

Working with clean hands, flatten out a level-tablespoon-sized portion of sausage in your palm. Place an olive in the center, then shape the sausage around it, enclosing the olive. Roll the sausage-wrapped olive in the bread crumbs, continuing to shape it and pressing the crumbs into the sausage. Repeat with the remaining olives. As olives are prepared, arrange them, spaced apart, on the baking sheet.

The poppers can be prepared to this point up to 1 day in advance, covered tightly, and refrigerated.

At least 20 minutes before baking, preheat an oven to 450 degrees F. Bake the olives for about 12 to 14 minutes, until the sausage is cooked and lightly browned. Serve in a long olive tray or speared on fun picks.

☛ TIP   You can also make these using panko Japanese bread crumbs or finely grated fresh bread crumbs.

APPETIZERS

139

Bollywood Chicken Skewers
with Spiced Yogurt Dip

Toasted Indian spices and lots of green herbs set these skewers apart. The spiciness of fresh jalapeños varies greatly, so take a tiny taste to gauge the heat, then adjust to your preference. The yogurt dip provides a cooling contrast.

2 pounds boneless, skinless chicken breasts

RUB

6 tablespoons olive oil

3 tablespoons finely chopped white onion

2 teaspoons minced fresh garlic

2 teaspoons cumin seed

2 teaspoons black mustard seed

2 tablespoons fresh lime juice

1 to 2 teaspoons minced seeded fresh jalapeño

¼ cup coarsely chopped fresh parsley

2 tablespoons coarsely chopped fresh mint

¼ cup coarsely chopped fresh cilantro

1 teaspoon salt

¼ teaspoon freshly ground black pepper

1 tablespoon water

SPICED YOGURT DIP

½ cup nonfat plain yogurt

½ teaspoon ground coriander

¼ teaspoon ground cumin

½ teaspoon minced fresh garlic

30 six- to eight-inch bamboo skewers

FOR GARNISHING

Chopped fresh cilantro

1 lime, cut into wedges

Cut the chicken into ½-by-4-inch strips; you should have about 30 strips. Refrigerate in a large bowl until needed.

To make the rub: Heat 3 tablespoons of the oil in a small nonstick skillet or sauté pan over medium heat. Cook the onion, uncovered, stirring occasionally, for 4 to 5 minutes, or until deep brown. Do not let the onion scorch. Add the garlic and cumin and mustard seeds and sauté for 30 seconds. Do not brown the garlic.

Remove from the heat and mix in the lime juice, jalapeño, fresh herbs, salt, and pepper. Transfer the mixture to a food processor (a small one is best) and, with the machine running, drizzle in the remaining 3 tablespoons oil and the water and process to a paste-like consistency.

Add the rub to the chicken strips and mix well. Marinate, refrigerated, for at least 4 hours or preferably overnight.

Meanwhile, to make the spiced yogurt dip: Mix all the dip ingredients together in a small bowl until smooth. Refrigerate until ready to serve.

When ready to cook the chicken, soak the bamboo skewers in water for at least 1 hour. Prepare a medium-hot fire in a charcoal grill, or preheat a gas grill to medium-high. Oil the grill. Thread the chicken on the skewers. Grill for about 2 to 3 minutes per side, or until cooked through.

Serve the skewers on a platter, with the yogurt dip in a small bowl in the center, for guests to help themselves. Garnish with cilantro sprigs and lime wedges for squeezing.

☛ TIP   You can also bake the chicken. Preheat an oven to 475 degrees F. Spray two baking sheets with cooking spray or lightly oil them. Place the skewers, spaced apart, on the baking sheets, and bake for 8 to 10 minutes, or until cooked through.

Cha Cha Cashews

Sweet, salty, and slightly spicy, these addictively crunchy nuts keep for up to two weeks in a tightly sealed jar or tin.

> 1 egg white
> 1 tablespoon water
> 1 pound (about $3\frac{1}{2}$ cups) salted, roasted cashews
> $\frac{1}{3}$ cup sugar
> 1 tablespoon chili powder
> 2 teaspoons ground cumin
> 2 teaspoons ground coriander
> 2 teaspoons kosher salt
> $\frac{1}{2}$ teaspoon cayenne pepper

Preheat an oven to 250 degrees F. Spray a rimmed baking sheet with cooking spray, or lightly oil it, and set aside.

In a medium bowl, whisk the egg white and water until foamy. Add the cashews and toss to coat. Transfer the nuts to a strainer, shake, and let drain for about 2 minutes.

In a large bowl, mix the sugar, chili powder, cumin, coriander, salt, and cayenne. Add the nuts and toss to coat thoroughly.

Spread the nuts on the baking sheet in a single layer. Roast for 40 minutes. Stir the nuts with a spatula and spread them out again. Roast for 20 minutes longer, until the nuts are dry.

Using a spatula, loosen the nuts on the baking sheet but do not remove them. Let cool to room temperature. Be sure to let the nuts cool completely and become crisp. Store in an airtight container at room temperature for up to 2 weeks. If necessary, recrisp them in a 350 degree F oven for a few minutes before serving.

Bacon, Blue Cheese & Pecan
Cocktail Cookies

Yes . . . it's a bacon cookie! This cocktail companion will be everyone's new guilty pleasure.

- ¾ cup (about 2½ to 2¾ ounces) pecans
- 4 strips bacon, minced (you should have about ½ cup, packed)
- Salted butter, as needed to make ½ cup with bacon drippings
- 1 cup (about 4¾ ounces) crumbled blue cheese
- 1 teaspoon minced fresh thyme, or ¼ teaspoon dried
- ½ teaspoon freshly ground black pepper
- 1 cup all-purpose flour

Preheat an oven to 350 degrees F.

Spread the nuts on a rimmed baking sheet and bake until lightly toasted, about 5 to 6 minutes. Let cool, and then coarsely chop.

In a medium skillet or sauté pan over medium to medium-high heat, sauté the bacon until crispy, about 5 minutes; do not scorch. Drain the drippings into a heatproof measuring cup, and reserve the bacon separately. Let cool. To the cooled drippings, add butter as needed to make ½ cup total.

With an electric mixer, cream the cheese, thyme, and pepper together in a mixing bowl. Add the butter mixture and mix in well. Add the flour and mix the dough for about 2 minutes. Add the bacon and nuts and mix until just evenly combined. Refrigerate the dough for at least 30 minutes to chill.

Preheat an oven to 350 degrees F at least 20 minutes before baking. Line baking sheets with parchment paper or leave them ungreased.

Scoop up the dough by rounded teaspoonfuls and shape into 1-inch-diameter balls (you should get 36 to 40). Place, spaced 2 inches apart, on the baking sheets. With a fork, flatten to 1½-inch-diameter rounds, dipping the tines into flour as needed, and making crisscross patterns as you would on peanut butter cookies. Bake until lightly golden at the edges, about 14 to 16 minutes. Cool on the pan.

Coriander Citrus Shrimp
"Lollipops"

Large shrimp are curled into circles and skewered to form "lollipops" before roasting in a hot oven. This preparation is very healthful and low in fat but full flavored.

MARINADE

1 tablespoon ground coriander

2 tablespoons orange juice concentrate

3 tablespoons olive oil

1 tablespoon very finely minced orange zest

2 tablespoons fresh lime juice

1 tablespoon minced fresh garlic

2 teaspoons Dijon mustard

1/4 cup chopped cilantro

1/2 teaspoon red pepper flakes

1/2 teaspoon salt

1 pound large (16 to 20 per pound) raw shrimp

16 to 20 six-inch bamboo skewers

FOR GARNISHING

Fresh cilantro sprigs

Lime wedges or wheels

To make the marinade: In a large bowl, mix the marinade ingredients until well combined.

Peel and devein the shrimp, and remove the tails. (Or purchase cleaned raw shrimp.) Add the shrimp to the marinade and stir to coat well. Cover and refrigerate for at least 1 hour, or up to 4 hours. Soak the skewers in water for at least 1 hour.

Preheat an oven to 450 degrees F. Spray a baking sheet with cooking spray or lightly oil it.

APPETIZERS

145

continued >

Skewer a shrimp, curled into a circle, on the tip of a skewer, so that it looks like a shrimp "lollipop." (Be sure to thread both head and tail ends of shrimp onto the skewer.) Repeat with remaining shrimp. As each skewer is done, lay it on the baking sheet, spacing the skewers apart, not touching. Spoon some of the marinade on top of each shrimp.

Roast the shrimp for about 5 minutes, or until just cooked through and pink. Serve the shrimp skewers on a platter and garnish with cilantro and lime.

Pineapple Avocado Salsa

MAKES ABOUT
5 CUPS

Scoop up this colorful tropical salsa with tortilla chips, Pita Crisps (page 162), or taro root chips. You can also substitute mango for half the pineapple.

¼ cup fresh lime juice

1 tablespoon honey

1 teaspoon kosher salt

Pinch of red pepper flakes or minced fresh jalapeño,
depending on spiciness desired

¼ cup minced red onion

3 cups finely chopped ripe fresh pineapple

½ cup finely diced red bell pepper (about 1 small pepper)

2 large ripe but firm avocados

½ cup coarsely chopped fresh cilantro

Have all ingredients, except the avocados, cut up and measured before assembling.

In a large bowl, mix the lime juice, honey, salt, and pepper flakes well. Add the onion, pineapple, and bell pepper.

Quarter and peel the avocados, then cut into small dice and add to the salsa along with the cilantro. Lightly and gently fold all the ingredients together until well combined. Refrigerate for up to 30 minutes before serving, or serve immediately. Serve in a bowl with a spoon on a platter surrounded by dippables.

Romesco Roasted Red Pepper
& Almond Spread

This earthy spread is excellent with manchego cheese, Spanish olives, and rustic flatbreads.

½ cup (1½ to 1¾ ounces) sliced almonds

½ cup sun-dried tomatoes in oil, drained and oil reserved separately

¼ teaspoon red pepper flakes

1 teaspoon minced fresh garlic

1 teaspoon very finely minced orange zest

Extra-virgin olive oil, if needed

¾ cup coarsely chopped roasted red peppers

1 tablespoon red wine vinegar

2 tablespoons fresh orange juice

¼ teaspoon salt

Preheat an oven to 375 degrees F.

Spread the almonds on a rimmed baking sheet, and bake for about 4 minutes or until golden and lightly toasted. Let cool.

In a food processor, combine the drained tomatoes, pepper flakes, garlic, orange zest, and cooled almonds. Process until smooth, about 1 minute.

Meanwhile, measure the oil drained from the tomatoes, and add extra-virgin olive oil as needed to make ¼ cup total. Add to the processor along with the roasted peppers, vinegar, orange juice, and salt, and continue processing until smooth.

The spread can be made up to 4 days in advance, covered, and refrigerated until needed. Let come to room temperature before serving.

Lamb "Sliders"
on Homemade Rosemary Buns

MAKES 24

Tiny "sliders" are so hot as an appetizer! Making the rosemary buns is a bit of work but is really worth it, and if you haven't baked bread before, the recipe is fairly straightforward. If you don't want to bake, you can serve the sliders on slices of hearty baguette. Also, for an outdoor party, you can grill the lamb, or if lamb is not your thing, you can substitute beef.

SPREAD

¾ cup mayonnaise, or use ⅜ cup mayonnaise and ⅜ cup plain yogurt

1½ tablespoons whole-grain mustard

1 tablespoon minced fresh garlic

BURGER MIXTURE

¾ teaspoon freshly ground black pepper

2 tablespoons Dijon mustard

2 teaspoons minced fresh rosemary

3 tablespoons minced onion

2 teaspoons minced fresh garlic

1 tablespoon balsamic vinegar

1½ teaspoons salt

1½ pounds ground lamb, or substitute beef

ACCOMPANIMENTS

24 Mini Rosemary Buns (page 150)

   or substitute high-quality purchased mini buns or sliced baguette

Thinly sliced red or sweet onions

Baby arugula or gourmet greens

To make the spread: Mix the ingredients together well. Cover and refrigerate, for up to 2 days, until needed.

continued >

To make the burger mixture: In a bowl, mix the pepper, mustard, rosemary, onion, garlic, vinegar, and salt. Mix in the lamb until thoroughly combined. Divide the mixture into 24 portions, about 1 heaping tablespoon each. Shape into patties, about 2 inches in diameter.

Heat a medium or large nonstick skillet or sauté pan over medium-high to high heat. Working in batches without crowding the pan, sauté the patties until just done, about 2 minutes per side.

If you want to serve the buns warm, wrap them in aluminum foil and reheat in a 375 degree F oven.

To serve, split the buns and spread with the mayonnaise mixture. Place the patties on buns and top with onions and arugula as desired. Close the burgers and secure with picks.

Mini Rosemary Buns

MAKES 24 MINI BUNS

DOUGH

$\frac{1}{2}$ cup whole milk

1 tablespoon salted butter

2 tablespoons sugar

$\frac{1}{2}$ teaspoon salt

1 ($\frac{1}{4}$-ounce) package active dry yeast

$\frac{1}{3}$ cup warm (105 to 115 degrees F) water

1 egg, whisked

2 teaspoons very finely minced fresh rosemary

2 cloves garlic, minced

2 tablespoons freshly grated Parmesan cheese

$2\frac{1}{2}$ cups all-purpose flour, plus more as needed for kneading the dough

EGG WASH

1 egg

1 tablespoon water

To make the dough: In a small saucepan over medium heat, bring the milk just to a simmer, remove from the heat, and stir in the butter, sugar, and salt. Stir to dissolve the sugar and salt, let cool to lukewarm, and pour into a large mixing bowl.

Meanwhile, in a small bowl, dissolve the yeast in the warm water, then add to the milk mixture. Stir in the egg, rosemary, garlic, and cheese. Mix in as much flour as needed to make a smooth moist dough.

On a clean, lightly floured surface, knead the dough until smooth. Transfer to a large oiled bowl, then turn dough over to oil the top. Cover with a nonfuzzy kitchen towel and let rise in a warm place until doubled, about 1½ hours.

Punch down and roll the dough into a log, 2 inches in diameter. Cut the log into quarters, then each quarter into 6 equal pieces. Roll into balls, then shape into 2-inch diameter disks. Lay out disks on a greased baking sheet, cover lightly with a towel, and let rise until almost doubled, about 20 to 30 minutes.

Meanwhile, preheat an oven to 375 degrees F.

To make the egg wash: In a small bowl, whisk the ingredients together.

Brush the tops of the buns lightly with egg wash. Bake the buns for about 9 to 12 minutes, until golden brown and cooked through.

If made ahead, cool thoroughly, then wrap in a plastic bag, and store at room temperature for up to 2 days. Wrap the buns in foil, and reheat in an oven before serving.

Chipotle Deviled Eggs

I've been making these for years and they have become a cocktail-party staple. The spicy tomato topping adds textural and visual pizzazz. They're great with Cheladas (page 61), Amante Picantes (page 35), or Cheaters Blended Margaritas (page 99).

1 dozen eggs

3 tablespoons regular or low-fat sour cream

3 tablespoons mayonnaise or reduced-fat mayonnaise

½ teaspoon salt

½ teaspoon Dijon mustard (optional)

1 to 2 tablespoons chipotle chile purée (see Tip)

1 teaspoon minced fresh garlic

2 tablespoons thinly sliced green onion, white and green parts

TOPPING

½ cup ¼-inch diced tomatoes

1 tablespoon minced white onion

2 tablespoons chopped fresh cilantro

1 to 2 teaspoons chipotle chile purée (see Tip)

Put the eggs in a large nonreactive saucepan and add cold water to 1 inch above the eggs. Bring to a boil over medium-high heat, then reduce heat and simmer for 10 minutes. Remove from the heat and run cool water over the eggs in the pan until they are cooled. When cool, carefully peel them under running water.

Halve the eggs lengthwise and transfer the yolks to a bowl. Set the egg white halves on a platter, cover, and refrigerate.

With a fork or potato masher, mash the yolks to a smooth consistency. Mix in the sour cream, mayonnaise, salt, mustard, if using, chipotle purée, and garlic until smooth. (You can also do this in a mixing bowl with a whip attachment.) Stir in the green onion. Spoon the mixture into a pastry bag fitted with a plain or large star tip, then pipe the mixture evenly into the egg white halves.

To make the topping: In a small bowl, mix the ingredients together. Top each egg half with about 1 teaspoon of the topping.

☛ T I P   To make chipotle chile purée, put 1 can (7 ounces) chipotle peppers in adobo sauce, with the sauce, in a food processor and purée until smooth. Freeze any extra purée for another use.

Olive Tapenade

This recipe can be doubled or quadrupled easily for large parties. Feel free to zip it up with a little finely minced anchovy or a touch of minced fresh herbs. Or switch out the ripe black olives for pitted green olives if you like to mix it up a bit.

2 tablespoons grated Parmesan cheese

1 tablespoon minced fresh garlic

2 tablespoons capers, drained

1 cup pitted kalamata olives, drained

$^3/_4$ cup pitted black ripe olives, drained

2 teaspoons red wine vinegar

2 tablespoons extra-virgin olive oil

In a food processor, process the cheese, garlic, and capers until smooth. Add the olives, vinegar, and oil. Process until finely chopped. Tapenade can be stored, covered and refrigerated, for up to 1 week.

Piccolo Caprese Picks
with Quick Basil Aioli

The beloved Italian salad goes mini-on-a-pick. Be sure to purchase ciliegine mozzarella balls—these are the tiny cherry-sized ones. Great served up with Sexy Olive Mix (page 162).

AIOLI

2 teaspoons minced fresh garlic

1 tablespoon fresh lemon juice

3 tablespoons finely chopped fresh basil

⅓ cup high-quality mayonnaise, such as Best Foods or Hellmann's

¼ cup extra-virgin olive oil

CAPRESE

24 cherry tomatoes (about 1 pint)

24 small fresh basil leaves

24 ciliegine mozzarella balls (these are the tiny ⅓-ounce balls), drained well

Kosher salt

Freshly ground black pepper

24 short bamboo or other fun picks

To make the aioli: In a small bowl, whisk together the garlic, lemon juice, and basil. Whisk in the mayonnaise until smooth. Gradually drizzle in the olive oil, whisking constantly, until emulsified. Cover and refrigerate until needed. The aioli can be made up to 3 days in advance.

To assemble the caprese: With a paring knife, halve each cherry tomato horizontally, being careful to keep the halves together. Then thread onto a pick in this order: a tomato top, a basil leaf, a mozzarella ball, and the tomato bottom. Be sure the cut sides of the tomato face toward the cheese. Repeat with remaining ingredients. Place on a platter and sprinkle with salt and pepper. Serve with the aioli in a bowl for dipping or drizzling.

Mini Scallion Biscuits with
Smoked Salmon Spread & Pickled Onions

The trick to these tiny fluffy biscuits is to not overhandle the dough: the more you touch it, the less fluff you will get. The salmon spread can be made up to two days in advance.

¾ cup thinly sliced 1½-inch-long pieces red onion

¼ cup seasoned rice vinegar

2 cups all-purpose flour

2 teaspoons baking powder

¾ teaspoon salt

¼ teaspoon dry mustard

¼ teaspoon freshly ground black pepper

6 tablespoons cold salted butter, cut into chunks

2 large green onions, white and green parts, minced (about ⅓ cup)

1 tablespoon minced fresh parsley

¾ cup milk, plus more as needed

Smoked Salmon Spread (recipe follows)

FOR GARNISHING

24 to 28 small fresh dill sprigs

Preheat an oven to 425 degrees F.

In a small bowl, toss the onion and vinegar together. Cover and set aside to marinate for at least 30 minutes or up to 4 hours. Drain the onion just before using.

In a large bowl, mix the flour, baking powder, salt, dry mustard, and pepper. With a pastry blender or two knives, cut in the butter, or rub it in with your fingers, until the size of small peas. Stir in the green onions and parsley. With a fork, lightly stir in enough milk to make a soft dough. (Start with ¾ cup milk, then add more only as needed, 1 tablespoon at a time.) Take care not to overmix the dough.

Turn the dough out onto a lightly floured surface. Lightly pat out to ¾-inch thickness, handling the dough as little as possible. Sprinkle the dough lightly with flour. Cut into 24 to 28 rounds with a 1½-inch biscuit cutter. (Do not twist the cutter when cutting the dough.) Place the biscuits, with sides touching, on an ungreased baking sheet.

Bake for about 14 to 16 minutes, until golden. Remove from the oven and let cool on the pan for about 10 minutes.

Split the biscuits in half horizontally. Spread the biscuit bottoms with about 1 rounded teaspoonful of the salmon spread, and top the spread with a little of the drained pickled onion and a dill sprig. Arrange the biscuits on a serving platter, replace the top halves of the biscuits, slightly askew, and serve immediately.

Smoked Salmon Spread

MAKES ¾ CUP

> ½ (4 ounce) package cream cheese, at room temperature
> 3 ounces thinly sliced cold-smoked salmon
> ½ teaspoon prepared horseradish
> 2 teaspoons fresh lemon juice
> ½ teaspoon finely minced fresh dill

In a food processor, combine the cream cheese and half of the salmon and process until smooth. Add the horseradish and lemon juice, and process, scraping down the sides as necessary, until smooth. Add the dill and process until incorporated.

Transfer the spread to a small bowl. Finely chop the remaining salmon and stir it into the spread until evenly distributed. The salmon spread can be made up to 2 days in advance, and refrigerated, covered. Bring to room temperature before serving.

Seared Thai Beef Lettuce Cups
with Lemongrass & Lime

Interactive, or "build your own," is a popular style of app'ing today. If you have a large wok, serve the beef right from it on the table, set out the garnishes, and let guests assemble their own as described below.

1 pound beef tenderloin or tenderloin trim

MARINADE

2 tablespoons very finely minced peeled fresh ginger

2 tablespoons minced fresh garlic

2 tablespoons very finely minced fresh lemongrass, white part only

4 large kaffir lime leaves, minced

¼ cup sugar

3 tablespoons fish sauce

3 tablespoons fresh lime juice

2 tablespoons unseasoned rice vinegar

2 teaspoons Asian chili paste, such as sambal oelek

¼ cup peanut or other vegetable oil

1 teaspoon kosher salt

Peanut or other vegetable oil for sautéing

FOR GARNISHING

⅓ cup chopped salted peanuts

1 lime, cut into 8 wedges

Fresh cilantro sprigs

10 small leaves romaine-lettuce hearts

Trim the beef and cut into ½-by-1-by-1½-inch bite-sized pieces. Set aside in a bowl.

To make the marinade: Combine the ginger, garlic, lemongrass, lime leaves, and sugar in a food processor. Process for 1 minute, then add the remaining marinade ingredients and process for 1 minute more.

Add three quarters of the marinade to the beef and toss to coat well. Let marinate, refrigerated, overnight. Reserve the remaining marinade.

When ready to cook, drain the meat and discard the used marinade. Have the reserved marinade near the range. Heat a large heavy sauté pan or wok over high heat until very hot, almost smoking. Add 1 tablespoon of oil and heat until very hot but not smoking. Add half of the beef and cook until well browned but still rare to medium-rare, about 4 minutes. Let the beef get nice color, but turn it frequently with a spatula while cooking. Transfer to a platter and keep warm.

Cook the remaining beef, adding more oil as needed. Be sure to keep the pan very hot and cook the beef quickly. As soon as the last batch of beef is done, quickly add the reserved marinade to the hot pan.

Add the beef and heated marinade to the warm platter. Sprinkle with peanuts and garnish with the lime wedges and cilantro sprigs. Tuck the lettuce leaves around the sides. Serve immediately.

Instruct your guests to take a lettuce leaf, spoon in a couple pieces of beef with the sauce and peanuts, top with a few cilantro sprigs, and squeeze lime juice over all.

☛ TIPS   You can also grill the beef. Soak bamboo skewers in water for at least an hour, then thread 2 pieces of the marinated beef on each skewer. You should get about 20 skewers. Prepare a hot fire in a charcoal grill, or preheat a gas grill to high. Lightly oil the beef, and grill for about 2 minutes per side. When done, assemble the platter as described above, drizzling the skewers with the reserved marinade.

Alternatively, this recipe can be made with boneless, skinless chicken, cut as described. Cook the chicken until done, about 5 to 6 minutes if sautéing, or about 2½ minutes per side if grilling.

Greek Salsa with Pita Crisps

For a large crowd, this vibrant salsa can easily be multiplied. Since it's best made right before serving, I like to have everything ready in the fridge then mix it at the last minute.

SALSA

3 tablespoons extra-virgin olive oil

2 tablespoons fresh lemon juice

1½ teaspoons red wine vinegar

2 tablespoons chopped fresh oregano

¼ cup chopped fresh flat-leaf parsley

¼ teaspoon salt

1½ cups finely diced ripe plum tomato (about 3 tomatoes)

¾ cup finely diced, peeled, and seeded cucumber (about ½ cucumber)

¼ cup minced red onion

1½ teaspoons minced fresh garlic

1 small yellow bell pepper, seeded and finely diced

1 cup (about 4 ounces) crumbled feta cheese

⅓ cup pitted kalamata olives, finely chopped

2 to 3 pickled hot cherry peppers, stemmed and minced

Pita Crisps (page 162)

To make the salsa: Combine the salsa ingredients in a bowl and mix gently. Serve immediately with the pita crisps.

The salsa ingredients can be prepared a day in advance, refrigerated separately, then combined right before serving.

Pita Crisps

MAKES 96 CRISPS

6 large pocket-style pita breads (about 12 ounces total)
3 tablespoons olive oil
¾ teaspoon kosher salt

Preheat an oven to 450 degrees F.

Cut each pita into 8 triangles and then separate each triangle into 2 pieces. In a large bowl, combine the olive oil and salt. Add the pita wedges and toss well, coating them evenly with the oil mixture.

On two large baking sheets, spread out the pita wedges in a single layer. Bake for about 4 minutes, then turn the pieces over and continue baking for 4 to 5 more minutes more, or until golden and crisp.

The crisps can be made in advance, cooled, and stored in airtight containers for up to 3 days. If necessary, recrisp in a hot oven for a couple of minutes.

Sexy Olive Mix

MAKES 3 CUPS

With the proliferation of olive bars, you can "mix it up" with your olives for this recipe.

3 cups assorted olives, such as Greek olive mix, drained
1 tablespoon red wine vinegar
1 teaspoon minced fresh garlic
¼ teaspoon red pepper flakes
6 sprigs fresh thyme
1 sprig fresh rosemary, broken in half
Zest of ½ orange, removed in big pieces with a potato peeler
1 tablespoon extra-virgin olive oil

Combine all the ingredients in a nonreactive bowl and mix well. Cover and refrigerate for at least 12 hours so that flavors will marry before serving.

Creamy White Bean Dip
with Garlic & Rosemary

I like to serve this dip with Herbed Crostini (page 198), grilled rustic bread, fresh veggies—such as pieces of fennel bulb, red bell peppers, and blanched green beans— or grilled vegetables. For a variation, stir in chopped kalamata olives.

2 (15-ounce) cans white beans, drained well

6 cloves fresh garlic, peeled

½ teaspoon red pepper flakes

2 tablespoons fresh lemon juice

2 teaspoons very finely minced lemon zest

1½ teaspoons very finely minced fresh rosemary

¾ teaspoon kosher salt

½ cup extra-virgin olive oil

FOR GARNISHING

Extra-virgin olive oil

Fresh rosemary sprig

Combine the drained beans and garlic cloves in a food processor, and process for about 1 minute. Scrape down the sides of the bowl and add the pepper flakes, lemon juice and zest, rosemary, and salt. With the motor running, add the oil through the feed tube in a slow stream. Process until smooth. Taste for salt and adjust if desired. Store the dip, covered and refrigerated, for up to 3 days.

Serve the dip in a bowl, drizzle with a tiny bit of olive oil, and garnish with a fresh rosemary sprig.

APPETIZERS

163

Sassy Sherry-Roasted Peppers

Choose fairly thick-fleshed peppers, such as bell, Anaheim, cubanelle, pimiento, jalapeño, or cherry peppers. Serve over a log of goat cheese or with Creamy White Bean Dip with Garlic & Rosemary (page 163). Accompany with crostini, flatbread, or slices of crusty rustic bread.

3 pounds assorted, colorful sweet and hot peppers

¾ cup extra-virgin olive oil

¼ cup sherry vinegar

1 teaspoon kosher salt

2 tablespoons minced, mixed fresh herbs, such as basil, thyme, oregano, and flat-leaf parsley

Roast the peppers over a hot grill or coals, over a gas flame, under a broiler, or in a 500 degree F oven, turning often, until the skin is totally blistered and charred black. As the peppers are ready, transfer to a bowl and cover with plastic wrap to steam skins loose. Let cool until the peppers can be handled, about 15 to 20 minutes. Slip the skins off, then stem, seed, and cut the peppers into bite-sized rustic chunks. Put the peppers in a large bowl, add the remaining ingredients, and mix gently. Store, refrigerated, for up to 1 week. Or, if making a large batch when loads of pepper varieties are in season, divide the peppers evenly into jars or plastic freezer containers, topping each one with additional extra-virgin olive oil. Label and freeze for up to 1 year.

Grilled Bread
with Bruschetta Tomatoes

For any outdoor grilling event, make this "required" appetizer with local ripe organic tomatoes whenever possible.

3 tablespoons extra-virgin olive oil

3 cups chopped vine-ripe tomatoes (about 2 to 3 medium tomatoes)

¼ cup chopped fresh basil

2 tablespoons minced red onion or shallots

1½ teaspoons minced fresh garlic

¾ teaspoon kosher salt

1 loaf rustic artisanal bread

FOR GARNISHING

Freshly ground black pepper

Prepare a medium-hot fire in a charcoal grill, or preheat a gas grill to medium-high.

In a medium bowl, toss together 2 tablespoons of the olive oil, the tomatoes, basil, onion, garlic, and salt and set aside.

If using a large "fat" loaf of bread, cut six ½-inch-thick slices with a serrated knife, then halve each piece crosswise, to make 12 pieces. If using a baguette-style loaf, cut twelve ½-inch-thick slices from the loaf. Reserve the remaining bread for another purpose.

Brush both sides of the bread slices with the remaining olive oil, and grill on each side until lightly marked or toasted. Arrange on a platter and immediately top with the reserved tomato mixture. Garnish with pepper.

Sicilian Mini Meatballs

Mini meatballs are always a party hit. If time is tight, you can make these up to four days in advance, cover with the sauce, and reheat them right before serving. Be sure to accompany with small slices of rustic bread for sauce-dipping.

SAUCE

½ cup golden raisins

¼ cup white wine

¼ cup extra-virgin olive oil

½ cup chopped onion

¼ cup pine nuts

1 tablespoon minced fresh garlic

1 vine-ripened tomato, diced

1 (15-ounce) can tomato sauce

¼ teaspoon salt

MEATBALLS

1½ pounds ground veal, or substitute beef

2 tablespoons minced shallot

1 tablespoon minced fresh garlic

2 tablespoons chopped fresh basil

1 teaspoon salt

¼ teaspoon freshly ground black pepper

⅛ teaspoon ground nutmeg

1 egg

½ cup freshly grated bread crumbs

3 tablespoons whole milk

3 tablespoons grated Parmesan cheese

FOR GARNISHING

Fresh basil leaves

To make the sauce: In a small bowl, soak the raisins in white wine for 10 minutes. In a nonreactive small skillet or saucepan over medium-high heat, heat the oil until hot. Sauté the onion and pine nuts for 4 minutes. Add the garlic and diced tomato and sauté for 2 to 3 minutes. Stir in the soaked raisins, with any unabsorbed wine, and bring to a boil for 1 minute. Add the tomato sauce and salt, bring to a simmer, and cook gently, stirring frequently, for about 10 minutes, or until saucy. (If the sauce gets too thick, add a touch of water.) Keep warm, or if made ahead, reheat. If making ahead, cool, cover, and refrigerate for up to 4 days.

To make the meatballs: Preheat an oven to 400 degrees F. Spray a rimmed baking sheet with cooking spray, or lightly oil it, and set aside.

Combine the meatball ingredients in a large bowl and, with clean hands, mix thoroughly. Scoop up level tablespoon-sized portions (or I like to use a #70 scoop) and shape into small balls. Place the meatballs, spaced apart, on the baking sheet. Bake for about 8 minutes, or until lightly browned and cooked through.

Spoon half the sauce into a baking dish, pretty platter, or chafing dish. Add the hot meatballs, then spoon the remaining sauce over the top. Sprinkle with basil leaves.

Soy-Glazed Seared Tuna
on Green Onion Pancakes

This is my absolute favorite Asian appetizer served with a Sake Martini (page 70). It takes a bit of effort and pre-prep, but is worth it. You can make the sauces up to two days ahead. The day of serving, sear the tuna and make the pancakes; you can serve them either warm or at room temperature. Since this recipe is a bit involved, I suggest reading it all the way through before starting.

TUNA

8 to 10 ounces loin-cut ahi tuna (ask your fishmonger for a nice piece about 1½ to 2 inches in diameter)

1½ teaspoons vegetable oil

PANCAKES

⅔ cup all-purpose flour

1 teaspoon baking powder

½ teaspoon salt

1 teaspoon sugar

1 egg

⅓ cup whole milk

3 tablespoons chilled soda water

1 tablespoon minced sweet pickled ginger (sushi-style ginger)

⅔ cup thinly sliced green onions, white and green parts

1½ teaspoons black sesame seed

Vegetable oil for cooking

Wasabi Mayo (page 171)

Soy Glaze (page 171)

FOR GARNISHING

Thinly sliced green onion tops

Black sesame seed

continued >

To cook the tuna: Heat a medium nonstick skillet over high heat until very hot. Rub the tuna with the oil and blot off any excess. Wipe the pan with oil to leave just a film, not a pool of oil, in the pan. Sear the tuna for about 45 seconds to 1 minute per side. Do not overcook the center. Tuna is best when rare to medium-rare. Set the tuna on a plate and set aside while cooking the pancakes.

To make the pancakes: In a small bowl, whisk together the flour, baking powder, salt, and sugar. In a medium bowl, whisk together the egg, milk, and soda water. Mix the flour mixture into the egg mixture, then mix in the ginger, green onions, and 1½ teaspoons sesame seed.

Heat your favorite pancake pan over medium to medium-high heat. To test the griddle's readiness, sprinkle with a few drops of water. If they "skittle around," the heat should be just about right. If needed, drizzle about 1 teaspoon or so of vegetable oil in the pan, then wipe with a paper towel to lightly oil the surface and remove any extra grease.

For each pancake, drop 1 heaping tablespoon of batter onto the heated griddle. Cook the pancakes in small batches. Turn the pancakes when they are set, slightly puffy, and lightly golden on the first side, about 1½ minutes. Cook until just browned on the second side and cooked through, about 1½ minutes more. As the pancakes are done, transfer to a plate lined with a paper towel, then cook the remaining pancakes.

To serve, cut the tuna into 16 slices, about ¼-inch thick. Lay a slice on each pancake, then top with 1 teaspoon of wasabi mayo and drizzle with about 1 teaspoon of soy glaze. Sprinkle each pancake with green onion and black sesame seed for garnish.

Wasabi Mayo

2 teaspoons wasabi powder or 1 tablespoon wasabi paste, or to taste

2 teaspoons water

$\frac{1}{3}$ cup mayonnaise

$\frac{1}{4}$ teaspoon sugar

Mix the wasabi powder and water and let sit 5 minutes. (If using wasabi paste, you do not need to let it sit.) Mix in the mayonnaise and sugar. Cover and refrigerate, for up to 1 week, until needed.

Soy Glaze

$\frac{1}{2}$ cup soy sauce

2 tablespoons sugar

$1\frac{1}{2}$ teaspoons cornstarch

Whisk all the ingredients together in a small saucepan, then, whisking frequently, bring to a boil over medium-high heat to thicken. Or, whisk all ingredients together, put in a microwavable dish, and cook on high until the mixture boils and thickens. Let cool. Cover and refrigerate, for up to 1 week, until needed. The recipe makes more than needed for the tuna; use the extra on grilled fish, chicken, or veggies.

APPETIZERS

171

Orange-Pistachio Cocktail Cookies | MAKES 24 TO 30

Studded with colorful pistachios, these savory bites are not only beautiful to look at but, with their exotic trace of orange blossom, they're elegant in taste, too. Sample one with a Vesper (page 70), a Lillet-perfumed martini.

1 cup (4 ounces) raw shelled pistachios
6 tablespoons salted butter, at room temperature
¾ cup (3¾ ounces) crumbled feta cheese
2 tablespoons sugar
1 tablespoon very finely minced orange zest
1 teaspoon orange flower water
¾ cup all-purpose flour
½ cup semolina flour
1½ tablespoons whole milk
Kosher salt for sprinkling

Preheat an oven to 325 degrees F.

Spread the nuts on a rimmed baking sheet and roast until lightly toasted, about 5 minutes. Let cool, then coarsely chop. Set aside.

In a mixing bowl, cream together the butter, cheese, sugar, orange zest, and orange flower water with an electric mixer until light and fluffy. In a separate bowl, mix the flours. Add the flour mixture to the creamed mixture and mix well, stopping and scraping down the sides of the bowl as necessary. Add the milk and mix until incorporated. Mix in the in reserved nuts.

Divide the dough in half and shape into logs, 6 inches long and 1½ inches in diameter. Wrap tightly in plastic wrap, twisting the ends, to help firm the dough. Chill in the refrigerator for 2 hours or in the freezer for about 30 minutes to further firm the dough. (The dough can be kept frozen for up to 1 month; remove from the freezer to temper overnight in the refrigerator before slicing.)

Preheat an oven to 325 degrees F at least 20 minutes before baking. Line baking sheets with parchment paper or spray them with cooking spray.

Cut the dough into ¼-inch-thick rounds and place about 1 inch apart on the baking sheets. Sprinkle lightly with salt. Bake for about 12 to 14 minutes, until cookies are lightly golden on the bottom and still pale on top. Let cool.

Fennel-Roasted Walnuts

MAKES 5 CUPS

These savory salty-sweet nuts can be habit-forming! Put out bowls for nibbling with an Italian-inspired Preso cocktail (page 55).

    2 tablespoons fennel seed
    ⅓ cup sugar
    2 teaspoons kosher salt
    ¼ teaspoon freshly ground black pepper
    1 egg white
    1 pound (about 4 cups) walnut halves

Preheat an oven to 250 degrees F. Spray a rimmed baking sheet with cooking spray, or lightly oil it.

Grind the fennel seed in a spice grinder or mortar and pestle until finely ground. In a large bowl, mix the ground fennel with the sugar, salt, and pepper. Set aside.

In a large bowl, whisk the egg white until frothy. Add the nuts and toss to coat evenly. Using a fine-mesh strainer, drain off excess egg white. Add the drained nuts to the spice mixture and stir to coat evenly.

Spread the nuts on the pan; they will be a little thicker than a single layer. Roast for 20 minutes. Stir, and roast for 20 minutes more, until the nuts are golden and crisp. Remove from the oven and stir the nuts on the baking sheet but do not remove them. Be sure to let the nuts cool completely and become crisp. Store in an airtight container at room temperature for up to 2 weeks. If necessary, recrisp them in a 350 degree F oven for a few minutes before serving.

Prosciutto Scallop Pops
with Lemon Artichoke Pesto

For a striking presentation, you can remove the picks fastening the prosciutto and replace them with long rosemary sprigs. The scallops are equally delicious sautéed; just be sure to have your pan very hot and not to crowd it. The lemon artichoke pesto is also luscious as a topping on crostini or with salmon.

3 ounces thinly sliced (not shaved) prosciutto, about 3 to 6 slices, depending on size of prosciutto

12 medium (1- to 1½-inch-diameter) scallops

12 wooden pupu picks or toothpicks

Olive oil for grilling

Salt

Freshly ground black pepper

Lemon Artichoke Pesto (recipe follows), at room temperature

FOR GARNISHING

Rosemary sprigs

Cut each slice of prosciutto into 2 to 4 lengthwise strips, making 12 strips total. (These will need to fit around the scallops, so think about this when cutting.)

Wrap a strip of prosciutto around the circumference of each scallop and secure with a pick. Cover and refrigerate until ready to cook. Remove scallops from the refrigerator about 20 to 30 minutes before cooking.

When ready to serve, prepare a hot fire in a charcoal grill, or preheat a gas grill to high. Spread 1 tablespoon of olive oil on a platter or tray. Lay the scallops in the oil; turn to oil both sides. Season each side lightly with salt and pepper to taste.

Placing the scallop surfaces down on the grill, cook the scallops for about 1½ to 3 minutes per side, depending on their size and the heat of your grill. There should be nice char marks on the surface, with the scallops still translucent in center. Do not overcook.

Serve on small plates with a dollop of the pesto or on a platter with the pesto in a small bowl. Garnish with rosemary.

Lemon Artichoke Pesto

MAKES 1½ CUPS

>1 (13¾-ounce) can artichoke hearts or quartered hearts, drained
>1 tablespoon lemon juice
>1 tablespoon minced fresh garlic
>Pinch of red pepper flakes, or substitute cayenne pepper
>2 tablespoons extra-virgin olive oil
>1 tablespoon capers, drained well
>2 teaspoons very finely minced lemon zest
>3 tablespoons basil pesto
>3 tablespoons chopped fresh flat-leaf parsley
>½ teaspoon very finely minced fresh rosemary

Combine the artichokes, lemon juice, garlic, pepper flakes, oil, capers, lemon zest, and pesto in a food processor, and pulse a few times until the mixture is chunky— like a salsa consistency. Stir in the fresh herbs. If made ahead, cover and refrigerate for up to 2 days. Bring to room temperature before serving.

Asian Shrimp Cakes
with Sweet Chili Sauce

These cakes are fantastic to whip up for a cocktail party because they are quick-roasted in the oven, so you won't be tied to a sauté pan. For a tasty variation, place the shrimp cakes on thin slices of English cucumber. Team with Zen Turkey Dumplings with Peanut Sauce (page 192) for a dynamic duo.

1½ teaspoons cornstarch
1 tablespoon soy sauce
1 tablespoon fresh lime juice
1 tablespoon Thai sweet chili sauce
1 tablespoon minced fresh garlic
1 tablespoon very finely minced peeled fresh ginger
1 egg white
2 tablespoons chopped fresh cilantro
2 green onions, white and green parts, thinly sliced
1 pound large raw peeled and deveined shrimp
¼ cup finely diced carrot

FOR GARNISHING
6 tablespoons Thai sweet chili sauce
Fresh cilantro leaves

In a medium bowl, mix the cornstarch, soy sauce, lime juice, and 1 tablespoon chili sauce until smooth. Stir in the garlic, ginger, egg white, chopped cilantro, green onions, and half the shrimp. Transfer the mixture to a food processor and process for about 20 seconds, until the mixture is coarsely pureed but not a paste.

Chop the remaining shrimp into ¼-inch to ⅓-inch pieces. Add the shrimp and diced carrot to the mixture, and pulse in just to mix evenly. The recipe can be made to this point, covered, and refrigerated, for up to 1 day in advance.

When ready to cook the shrimp cakes, preheat an oven to 450 degrees F. Thoroughly oil a baking sheet or spray well with cooking spray.

Scoop up heaping tablespoonfuls of the shrimp mixture, and place, spaced apart, on the baking sheet. Lightly press the mixture to spread cakes to 1½ inches in diameter.

Bake for about 4 minutes, turn the cakes, then bake for about 4 minutes more, until cakes are browned on both sides and just cooked through.

Serve immediately on a platter and top each shrimp cake with about ¾ teaspoon of sweet chili sauce for garnish. Scatter with cilantro leaves.

D'Lish Peppadew Peppers

MAKES 45 TO 50

With minimal ingredients, this simple snack is super-quick to make. If you don't have a pastry bag, pipe the filling from a small heavy-duty plastic sandwich bag with a corner cut off.

1 (14-ounce) jar Peppadew piquanté peppers (see Tip)
3 ounces fresh goat cheese (chèvre), at room temperature
1 (3-ounce) package cream cheese, at room temperature
45 to 50 whole Marcona fried almonds (about ⅓ cup)

FOR GARNISHING
Chopped fresh parsley

Drain the peppers thoroughly. Meanwhile, in a food processor or mixing bowl, combine the cheeses and mix until smooth. Fit a pastry bag with a plain tip, fill with the cheese mixture, and pipe into the peppers. Insert an almond into each pepper and sprinkle with parsley.

☛ TIP If you can't find jars of these peppers, check in the bulk olives section of a high-end grocery store for fresh-pack Peppadew peppers. For this recipe, you should purchase ¾ to 1 pound of the bulk peppers.

Sake Teriyaki Sticky Chicken Wings

Old-school teriyaki chicken wings get a big-flavored lacquery glaze in this low-and-slow method. You can make the sauce a few days ahead of time, but be sure to allow a full hour for cooking the wings.

¾ cup soy sauce

¼ cup sake, or substitute dry sherry or dry white wine

2 tablespoons very finely minced peeled fresh ginger

1 tablespoon minced fresh garlic

¾ cup sugar

1 teaspoon red pepper flakes

¼ cup thinly sliced green onions, white and green parts

3 tablespoons unseasoned rice vinegar

3 tablespoons cornstarch

3 tablespoons water

1 dozen whole chicken wings or 2 dozen drummettes,
about 2½ to 3 pounds

FOR GARNISHING

2 tablespoons toasted sesame seed

Thinly sliced green onion tops

In a small saucepan, whisk together the soy sauce, sake, ginger, garlic, sugar, pepper flakes, green onions, vinegar, cornstarch, and water. Set the pan over medium heat and bring to a boil, whisking constantly, to thicken. Mixture will be very thick. Let cool. If not using immediately, store, covered and refrigerated, for up to 4 days.

If using whole wings, disjoint the wings and remove and discard tips; you should have 24 pieces. Put them in a large bowl and set aside.

continued >

Preheat an oven to 375 degrees F.

Add the sauce mixture to the bowl with the chicken and mix well to coat the chicken evenly. Spray a 9-by-13-inch baking dish with cooking spray or lightly oil it. Arrange the drummettes and sauce in a single layer in the dish.

Bake for 30 minutes. Stir and turn the chicken pieces over and bake for 20 minutes more. Stir and turn the chicken pieces again and bake for 10 minutes more, or until chicken is tender and sauce is thick and glazy. Total cooking time should be about 1 hour.

Stir the drummettes in the sauce once more, then transfer the chicken to a serving platter. Spoon some of the extra sauce over the chicken, then sprinkle with the sesame seed and green onions for garnish.

Oysters on the Half Shell
with Citrus Splash

Sweet and tart bits of citrus are a terrific contrast to briny oysters. When serving freshly shucked oysters on a buffet, lay them on pine or spruce boughs for a stunning presentation. Depending on your guests' tastes, count from 3 to 6 oysters per person.

Fresh oysters, in the shell

SPLASH

1 pink grapefruit

1 tangerine

1 small shallot, minced

1 tablespoon Champagne vinegar or white wine vinegar

1 tablespoon minced fresh chives

1/4 teaspoon red pepper flakes

Rinse the oysters and scrub the shells with a vegetable brush to remove any debris. Refrigerate, wrapped in a damp towel, until ready to shuck.

To make the splash: With a sharp knife, peel the grapefruit and tangerine just deep enough to expose the fruit, removing all white pulp. Section the citrus over a bowl to catch the juices, then finely chop the fruit sections. Put the fruit in the bowl, and add remaining ingredients.

Right before serving, shuck the oysters, discarding the top shells. Inspect the oysters for any bits of broken shell, picking them out carefully.

Set the oysters on a platter spread with crushed ice. Set the splash out in a small bowl so that guests can spoon a little over each oyster.

Mushroom & Fontina Purses

The filling for these is fairly "dry," so the purses can be assembled in the morning and then baked right before serving. The filling recipe can easily be doubled to use a full package of puff-pastry dough. The purses are baked at the same temperature as the Coriander Citrus Shrimp "Lollipops" (page 145), so, if you're serving both items, you can keep your oven on one temperature. And both are great right out of the oven but also tasty when they cool off, so don't feel that they need to stay hot on the table. They will be gobbled up in no time anyway.

FILLING

2 tablespoons olive oil

3 cups (about 6 ounces) chopped cremini mushrooms or
  wild mushrooms (see Tip)

2 teaspoons minced fresh garlic

1$\frac{1}{2}$ teaspoons minced fresh thyme

$\frac{1}{2}$ teaspoon salt

Pinch of freshly ground black pepper

$\frac{1}{4}$ cup dry sherry

$\frac{1}{2}$ cup (3 ounces) ricotta cheese

1 egg yolk

$\frac{1}{2}$ cup (2 ounces) coarsely grated fontina cheese

1 (10-by-10-inch) sheet Pepperidge Farm puff pastry
  (half of a 17.3-ounce package), thawed according to package directions

FOR GARNISHING

Fresh thyme sprigs

To make the filling: Heat the oil in a large nonstick sauté pan or skillet over high heat. Sauté the mushrooms for about 4 minutes, or until golden and tender. Add the garlic, thyme, salt, and pepper and sauté for 30 seconds. Add the sherry and cook until mushrooms are "dry," about 1$\frac{1}{2}$ minutes. Remove from heat and let cool.

Meanwhile, in a medium bowl, whisk the ricotta and egg yolk until well combined. Stir in the cooled mushrooms and then the fontina cheese. Cover and refrigerate, for up to a day, until ready to fill pastry.

To fill the pastry, lay out the sheet of puff pastry. Cut it lengthwise into 4 equal strips, then cut each strip crosswise into 4, making 16 squares. With a fork, poke each square 6 to 8 times, "docking" the dough. Place 1 level tablespoon of filling in the center of each square, using all the filling. With water-moistened fingertips, pull two opposite corners of a dough square together in the middle, pinching together to seal. Then pull the remaining opposite corners together and pinch to seal again. The pastry should make a little purse. Repeat with the remaining squares.

Arrange the purses, spaced apart, on a greased baking sheet. At this point, the purses can be covered and refrigerated for up to 12 hours.

When ready to bake, preheat an oven to 450 degrees F at least 20 minutes in advance.

Bake for about 14 minutes or until golden and crisp. Arrange on a platter and scatter with thyme sprigs. Serve immediately.

☛ TIP   If fresh chanterelle, porcini, or morel mushrooms are available, they would be delicious to use. If you are using cremini mushrooms and want to enhance them with some wild mushroom flavor, you can add 1 tablespoon of porcini powder to the sautéed mushrooms at the end of cooking when you add the sherry.

California Crab "Truffles"

These "truffles" are really cute and fun to make. The components take off from California sushi rolls. The truffles are a little time-consuming but worth the effort because they can be made the day before. The bite of avocado in the center is a great textural surprise—especially against the pop of the tobiko. Try to get an assortment of the flying fish roe—you can use regular golden tobiko, wasabi green, or spicy red!

1 (8-ounce) package cream cheese, at room temperature

1 tablespoon soy sauce

1 to 2 teaspoons Asian chili paste or wasabi paste, depending on
    how spicy you like it

½ cup finely diced, seeded, unpeeled English cucumber

1 pound fresh King, Dungeness, or lump crabmeat, drained well and
    picked through for shell fragments (if using King crab, chop coarsely)

1 ripe but firm avocado

6 ounces tobiko (flying fish roe)

FOR GARNISHING
Long pieces of fresh chives

In a mixing bowl, combine the cream cheese, soy sauce, and chili paste to taste and mix until well combined. Add the cucumber and crab, and stir in to combine well, but do not overmix. Refrigerate the mixture for at least 2 hours to chill thoroughly.

When the mixture is chilled, peel the avocado and cut into fifty ⅓-inch pieces (about the size of a large pea). Set aside. Place the tobiko in a small bowl and set aside.

Measure out 1 heaping teaspoonful of the crab mixture into the palm of your hand. Press an indentation into it with your thumb and insert a piece of the avocado. Roll into a ball, enclosing the avocado, and then roll in the tobiko, coating well and making a firm, well-formed ball. Repeat with the remaining ingredients. Place the truffles in a single layer in a container, preferably glass or plastic, such as a large glass baking dish. Cover and refrigerate for at least 1 hour, or up to overnight, until ready to serve.

To serve, place the truffles in straight lines on a serving platter or plate. I like to strew long pieces of chives on long white platters before setting down the truffles. If you use more than one kind of tobiko, alternate the colors in each row.

"Cocktail Shrimp"
with Martini Aioli

Jumbo shrimp are cooked with all the components of a gin martini to impart a total martini flavor. The aioli captures the garnishes: pimento-stuffed olives, lemon, and pickled cocktail onions.

$\frac{1}{2}$ cup dry white vermouth

$\frac{1}{4}$ cup gin

2 teaspoons juniper berries, crushed

Pinch of salt

Pinch of freshly ground black pepper

1$\frac{1}{2}$ pounds large raw peeled and deveined shrimp (16 to 20 per pound)

Martini Aioli (facing page)

FOR GARNISHING

Fresh flat-leaf parsley leaves or fresh chives

Lemon wedges or wheels

In a medium or large pot with a tight-fitting lid, combine the vermouth, gin, juniper berries, salt, and pepper. Over high heat, bring to a quick boil. Stir in the shrimp, cover, and steam for 1 minute. Remove the lid and stir the shrimp. Replace the lid and cook until shrimp are a little more than three-quarters cooked, about $\frac{1}{2}$ to 1 minute more. Remove from heat and let the shrimp cool in the cooking mixture, stirring occasionally, to finish cooking. Cool the shrimp, in the liquid, in the refrigerator until well chilled.

Serve in small martini glasses. Place a dollop of aioli in the center of each glass, then hang a few drained shrimp off the rim. Or, if you have a great collection of shot glasses, place a drained shrimp in a shot glass and dollop with aioli. Garnish with herbs and lemon.

Or arrange the shrimp on a platter, with the aioli in a small bowl in the center. Garnish with herbs and lemon.

Martini Aioli

2 tablespoons fresh lemon juice

2 raw egg yolks

1 tablespoon minced fresh garlic

1 teaspoon juniper berries, crushed and finely chopped

2 teaspoons minced lemon zest

½ teaspoon salt

1 teaspoon Dijon mustard

Pinch of cayenne pepper

1 cup vegetable oil

1 tablespoon gin

⅓ cup pimiento-stuffed green olives, drained well and minced

⅓ cup cocktail onions, drained well and minced

1 tablespoon finely chopped fresh flat-leaf parsley

In a food processor, combine the lemon juice, egg yolks, garlic, juniper berries, lemon zest, salt, mustard, and cayenne and process to combine thoroughly. With the processor running, gradually drizzle in the oil, emulsifying the aioli. The consistency should be thick and smooth, like mayonnaise. Add the remaining ingredients and pulse in. If not using immediately, cover and refrigerate, for up to 4 days, until needed.

Creole Crab "Cupcakes"

This is just about the cutest appetizer I have ever seen. The cupcakes were inspired by a recipe from chef friend Seis Kamimura. Serve warm or at room temperature.

CUPCAKES

2 tablespoons salted butter

⅓ cup ⅛-inch-diced onion

⅓ cup ⅛-inch-diced celery

⅓ cup ⅛-inch-diced red bell pepper

½ cup cornmeal

6 tablespoons all-purpose flour

1 tablespoon sugar

1¼ teaspoons baking powder

2 teaspoons Old Bay seasoning

1 egg

¼ cup whole milk

¼ cup sour cream

8 ounces fresh Dungeness or lump crabmeat, drained well and picked through for shell fragments

FROSTING

1 (3-ounce) package cream cheese, at room temperature

1 tablespoon milk

2 teaspoons fresh lemon juice

FOR GARNISHING

2 tablespoons thinly sliced chives

continued >

To make the cupcakes: Preheat an oven to 350 degrees F. Spray nonstick mini-muffin tins with cooking spray or lightly oil them. (The muffin tin cups should be 1¾ to 2 inches in diameter.) Set aside.

In a large sauté pan or skillet over medium heat, melt the butter and sauté the onion, celery, and bell pepper for about 3 to 4 minutes, until just starting to get tender. Let cool.

Meanwhile, in a small bowl, whisk together the cornmeal, flour, sugar, baking powder, and Old Bay. In a large bowl, whisk together the egg, milk, and sour cream.

When the sweated vegetables are cool, add the cornmeal mixture to the egg mixture, and mix lightly. Stir in the vegetables and all the melted butter from the pan, but do not overmix. Fold in the crabmeat just until evenly distributed.

Spoon a heaping tablespoon of batter into each muffin cup. You should fill 20 cups. Bake the cupcakes for about 12 to 14 minutes, or until a toothpick inserted in cupcake centers comes out clean. Rotate the pans after the first 7 to 8 minutes of baking.

Let the cupcakes cool in the pan for about 5 minutes, then carefully remove them from the pan and let cool briefly on a wire rack before frosting. The cupcakes can be made up to 1 day in advance, covered, and refrigerated before frosting. Refrigeration is imperative as the crab perishes swiftly if left at room temperature for an extended period of time. Bring to room temperature or warm for a minute or so in the oven before frosting.

To make the frosting: In a small bowl, mash the cream cheese with a fork, then whisk in the milk and lemon juice until smooth and creamy. Top each cupcake with about 1 teaspoon of frosting, then sprinkle with about ¼ teaspoon of chives for garnish.

Warm Brie & Almond Crostini
with Harvest Apple Chutney

I love the tangy chutney against the gooey cheese and the crispy nuts. You can prepare the recipe, up to the point of baking, up to a day ahead, cover well, and refrigerate.

CHUTNEY

1 large green apple, cored and cut into chunks

¼ cup chopped white onion

1 tablespoon salted butter

1 teaspoon very finely minced peeled fresh ginger

2 teaspoons cider vinegar

⅓ cup red pepper jam or red jalapeño jelly

1 tablespoon dried currants, or substitute chopped raisins

1 small (8-ounce) wheel brie cheese

20 to 24 ¼-inch-thick diagonal slices rustic skinny baguette

¾ cup (2½ ounces) sliced almonds, with skins

3 tablespoons thinly sliced fresh chives

In a food processor, pulse the apple and onion until they are chopped into ¼- to ⅓-inch pieces.

In a medium skillet or sauté pan, melt the butter over medium-high heat. Sauté the apple, onion, and ginger for 2 to 3 minutes, or until the apple and onion are just tender. Add the vinegar, jam, and currants and bring to a boil. Let the mixture boil for about 2 minutes, until loose and chutney-like. Let cool.

Preheat an oven to 450 degrees F. Spray a baking sheet with cooking spray, or lightly oil it, and set aside.

Cut the brie into ¼-inch-thick slices, sized to cover about three quarters of a baguette slice. Spread the almonds in a flat dish. Press the brie onto the bread slices, then the bread facedown into the almonds. Arrange faceup on the baking sheet. Bake until the brie is soft, and nuts are lightly toasted, about 4 to 5 minutes. Top each piece with a dollop of chutney and a sprinkle of chives. Serve immediately.

APPETIZERS

191

Zen Turkey Dumplings
with Peanut Sauce

If your friends like to get in the kitchen, they can be "hands-on" with this recipe. Extra helpers to assemble the dumplings are always welcome, especially if you arm your assistants with a Cucumber Elderflower Fizz (page 113) fortified with a shot of vodka!

1 tablespoon vegetable oil

$\frac{1}{2}$ cup minced stemmed fresh shiitake mushrooms (about 2 ounces before stemming)

2 tablespoons very finely minced peeled fresh ginger

2 tablespoons minced fresh garlic

1 teaspoon sugar

2 tablespoons soy sauce

2 tablespoons rice wine, or substitute dry sherry

2 teaspoons cornstarch

2 green onions, white and green parts, thinly sliced

8 ounces ground pork

8 ounces ground white turkey

1 (12-ounce) package wonton or gyoza wrappers, 40 to 50 pieces

Peanut Sauce (recipe follows)

FOR GARNISHING
Thinly sliced green onion tops

In a small skillet or sauté pan over medium-high heat, heat the oil until hot. Sauté the mushrooms, ginger, and garlic for about 2 to 3 minutes until the vegetables are sweated but not browned. In a medium bowl, whisk together the sugar, soy sauce, wine, and cornstarch. Add the green onions, pork, and turkey and mix well.

If you are not filling and steaming the dumplings right away, cover and refrigerate the filling for up to 1 day.

When ready to finish the dumplings, spray a metal or bamboo steamer insert with cooking spray or line it with lettuce or cabbage leaves. Set aside.

Lay out a wrapper on a clean work surface. With a fingertip dipped in water, very lightly moisten the corners. Put a level tablespoon of filling in the center. Fold two opposite corners across the filling, overlapping their points slightly. Draw up the remaining opposite corners and pinch together at center top, enclosing the filling. Repeat with the remaining wrappers and filling. Set the dumplings in the steamer insert, at least 1 inch apart. (You will have to steam the dumplings in batches, depending on the size of your steamer.)

Bring water to a boil in the steamer. Steam the dumplings for about 5 to 6 minutes, or until filling is firm and wrapper is tender. Serve the dumplings dolloped with peanut sauce, or serve the sauce alongside in a small bowl. (I like to serve the dumplings directly from the steamer.) Sprinkle with green onions for garnish.

Peanut Sauce

MAKES ABOUT ¾ CUP

> ⅓ cup creamy peanut butter
> ¼ cup soy sauce
> 1 tablespoon unseasoned rice vinegar
> 2 tablespoons sugar
> 1½ teaspoons minced fresh garlic
> 2 tablespoons hot water

In a small bowl, mix the ingredients together until smooth. The sauce can be made up to 3 days in advance. Serve warm or at room temperature.

Croque Monsieur Puffs

MAKES ABOUT 50

My current crush is this new incarnation of gougères, or cheese puffs. These were inspired by the classic French ham-and-cheese sandwich, Croque Monsieur. If you're serving only one thing with cocktails before dinner, it would have to be these heavenly puffs. They're perfect for "popping" in between sips of a Pear Thyme Fizz (page 48) or Peach 75 (page 72).

$\frac{1}{2}$ cup water

$\frac{1}{2}$ cup whole milk

6 tablespoons salted butter

$\frac{1}{2}$ teaspoon salt

$\frac{1}{2}$ cup minced ham

1 cup all-purpose flour

4 large eggs

$\frac{3}{4}$ cup (about 2$\frac{3}{4}$ ounces) grated Gruyère cheese

1 tablespoon chopped fresh chives

Adjust a rack to the middle of an oven and preheat to 400 degrees F.

Combine the water, milk, butter, salt, and ham in a heavy, medium saucepan. Bring to a boil over medium-high heat.

All at once, add the flour and stir in quickly with a wooden spoon. Keep stirring—the mixture will come away from the sides of the pan and become thick and stiff. Keep stirring and turning over for about 1 minute (you want it to dry out a bit).

Transfer the dough to an electric mixer, and turn mixer on medium-high speed. Add 1 egg and, as soon as it is partially incorporated, increase mixer speed to high. Add the remaining eggs, one at a time, when the previous egg is well incorporated. The mixture should be smooth. Mix in the cheese and chives.

If you have a strong arm, the dough can also be mixed by hand with a wooden spoon in a mixing bowl. Proceed as directed, and be sure to beat the dough until smooth before mixing in the cheese and chives. Let the mixture cool for about 10 minutes.

Meanwhile, line baking sheets with parchment paper or spray them with cooking spray. (Watch the puff bottoms closely to prevent over-browning if not using parchment.) By heaping teaspoonfuls, drop the mixture onto baking sheets in little balls, spaced apart. They should be the size of large marbles or jaw-breakers. (You can also use a pastry bag with a large plain tip to pipe them out.)

Bake for about 20 to 25 minutes, or until golden. Serve warm. (You can bake these a few hours in advance and reheat in a hot oven for a few minutes.)

Roasted Pear Crostini
with Gorgonzola

These are extra-delicious topped with chopped toasted nuts, such as hazelnuts or walnuts. Balsamic glaze can be purchased at gourmet and well-stocked grocery stores.

PEARS

2 firm red Bartlett or other red-skinned pears

1 tablespoon olive oil

1 tablespoon balsamic vinegar

1/4 teaspoon kosher salt

1 teaspoon minced fresh thyme

24 pieces Herbed Crostini (page 198)

1 cup (4 ounces) crumbled gorgonzola cheese or thinly sliced Cambozola

2 tablespoons balsamic glaze (see Tip page 198)

FOR GARNISHING

Tiny sprigs of fresh thyme

Preheat an oven to 450 degrees F.

To roast the pears: Quarter the pears lengthwise, then core. Cut each quarter lengthwise into 6 slices (you should have 24 slices, total). In a medium bowl, whisk together the oil, vinegar, salt, and thyme. Add the pears and toss to coat.

Spray a rimmed baking sheet with cooking spray. Lay out the pears, not touching, on the baking sheet. Roast for 12 to 15 minutes, or until golden and starting to caramelize on the edges. Pears can be cooled, covered, and refrigerated for up to 3 days before serving.

When ready to serve, lay out the crostini on a baking sheet and top each piece with about 1 heaping teaspoon of gorgonzola or a slice of Cambozola, then a slice of pear. Bake until just warmed, about 4 minutes.

Drizzle each piece with about 1/4 teaspoon balsamic glaze, then garnish with thyme.

Herbed Crostini

MAKES 32 TO 40 PIECES

Crostini are the must-have party basic. Use as a base for assorted toppers, such as creamy cheeses, tapenade, or spreads such as Romesco Roasted Red Pepper & Almond Spread (page 147).

> ⅓ cup olive oil
> ½ teaspoon dried basil leaves
> ½ teaspoon dried thyme leaves
> Pinch of cayenne pepper
> 1 teaspoon minced fresh garlic
> 1 long, skinny French baguette, cut into ¼-inch diagonal slices
> Kosher salt for sprinkling

In a small bowl, mix the oil, dried herbs, cayenne, and garlic. Lightly brush the baguette slices with the herb oil or, in a large bowl, drizzle the bread with the oil and toss well. Lay out the bread in a single layer on baking sheets, sprinkle with salt, and bake for about 8 to 10 minutes, until just crispy.

Crostini can be made in advance, cooled thoroughly, and stored in airtight containers for up to 3 days. If necessary, recrisp them in a hot oven for a couple of minutes.

☛ TIP Balsamic glaze is found in many well-stocked grocery stores and specialty food shops. If you are unable to find it then you can make it easily. In a small saucepan, combine ¾ cup balsamic vinegar and 2 tablespoons sugar, and bring to a simmer over medium-low heat. Reduce the heat to low and simmer for 10 to 12 minutes until the liquid is reduced to about ¼ cup or a light syrup texture. Watch carefully so as not to overreduce. Store, covered, at room temperature until needed.

Sources: Where The Pros Get It

AGAVE NECTAR Search the Web for multiple sites that carry this natural liquid sweetener made from wild agave. Or visit www.madhavahoney.com or www.blueagavenectar.com.

EDIBLE GLITTER Edible glitter is all-natural and is fun to sprinkle on cocktails. It comes in a variety of colors and is available at www.sugarcraft.com/catalog/flowers/glitter.htm.

EDIBLE GOLD AND SILVER Edible Gold Flake or Silver Flake comes in a clear shakable dispenser for easy use. Adds a touch of glamour when sprinkled on cocktails. Order at www.ediblegold.com.

DOUGLAS FIR TEA—JUNIPER RIDGE Wild Douglas fir tea and other forest-picked products are available at www.juniperridge.com.

FRUIT SYRUPS—MONIN PRODUCTS Producers of high-quality fruit syrups that are excellent in cocktails or nonalcoholic drinks. Visit www.moninathome.com for product info and ordering.

FRUIT PUREES—THE PERFECT PUREE OF NAPA VALLEY Delicious frozen fruit purees for signature drinks. Can be purchased by mail order at www.perfectpuree.com.

MUDDLERS AND HIGH-QUALITY BAR TOOLS—MR. MOJITO My favorite muddler comes from this online bar store. They offer lots of great variations on essential tools for the bar. Shop at www.mistermojito.com.

RESTAURANT, BAR, AND FOODSERVICE EQUIPMENT— BARGREEN ELLINGSON For restaurant and bar equipment, such as shakers, strainers, and large-quantity purchase of cocktail and martini glasses, visit their online store at www.bargreen.com.

Here is a sampling of my favorite items available from Bargreen Ellingson:

Citrus Zester (also known as a channel knife)—Mercer Tool, deep cutting zester, perfect for making long citrus-zest twists. Made of stainless steel with a plastic handle; MFR#: M15500

Cocktail Shaker—30 ounces Vollrath Deluxe mirror-finish stainless steel; MFR#: 46793.

Jiggers—Available in assorted sizes from American Metalcraft. Stainless steel and resistant to acids and fruit juices. Ounces stamped on each jigger.

Martini Glasses—My favorite martini glass comes from Libby. This 7½-ounce glass is the perfect size for a variety of drinks. Available 24 to a case. Libby; Bristol Valley Cocktail Glasses Code Number 8555SR.

Index

Hangover Helper

In the course of testing recipes for this book, I of course tried this one, too. And I am pleased to say that it works. Emergen-C gives you a C- and B-vitamin boost and replaces some lost electrolytes, vodka is a little "hair of the dog," bitters is a digestif, soda supplies bubbles, and the olive oil . . . well, an old bootlegger once told me that a small spoonful was good for coating a morning-after stomach. For a more substantial breakfast, "garnish" the drink with one strip of crispy-cooked bacon.

    1 packet raspberry- or orange-flavored Emergen-C
    1 ounce vodka
    2 dashes Angostura bitters
    4 ounces chilled soda water
    1 teaspoon extra-virgin olive oil (optional)

Empty the packet of Emergen-C into an old-fashioned or juice glass. Measure in the vodka. Add the bitters and soda water and stir. Top with olive oil, if using. Drink and feel better!